The

Rutgers Students Unofficial Guide to College

The
Rutgers Students
Unofficial
Guide to College

Michael Chodroff

Arm in Arm Publishing

The Rutgers Students Unofficial Guide to College
A Book of Bests and Worsts of Rutgers Students' Life at College

Compiled by Michael Chodroff

Published by:

Arm in Arm Publishing
Post Office Box 996
East Brunswick, NJ 08816-9998 U.S.A

Cover Design by Dave Leta
Printed in the United States of America by Book-mart Press

Library of Congress Card Number: 97-78206
ISBN: 0-9662801-0-5

DISCLAIMER

Rutgers, the State University of New Jersey is in no way affiliated with the contents of this book or the publishing of this book. This is the "unofficial" guide to Rutgers for the students and by the students. It is based on 1,067 surveys that were filled out and returned to Arm in Arm Publishing, Inc., by the students and alumni of Rutgers University. The lists in the books and the additional comments are based upon the responses that were provided in the returned surveys.

The author, publisher, the advertisers, and those institutions and products listed in this book do not necessarily agree with the opinions that are expressed in this book. This book was not compiled with the intent to harm anyone, rather to express the opinions of the Rutgers students and alumni for them and by them.

The purpose of this book is to entertain. The author and publisher shall have neither liability nor responsiblility to any person or entity with respect to any loss or damage caused, or alleged to be caused, directly or indirectly by the information contained in this book.

Although the author and publisher have exhaustively researched all sources to ensure the accuracy and completeness of the information contained in this book, we assume no responsiblity for errors, inaccuracies, omissions or any other inconsistency herein. Any slights against people or organizations are unintentional.

All brand names, product names, and business names used in this book are trademarks, registered trademarks, or trade names of their respective holders.

This book is dedicated to all the
friends, professors, and student
and faculty acquaintances that
helped make my four years at Rutgers
four of the best years of my life.
And for those that didn't - this book
is for you too.

CONTENTS

IV. FOOD

V. SOCIAL LIFE

VI. SPORTS

VII. NEW BRUNSWICK LIFE

VIII. LIFE ON CAMPUS

ACKNOWLEDGEMENTS

"Education is not
preparation for life,
education is life itself."

-John Dewey

"I pay the schoolmaster,
but 'tis the schoolboys
that educate my son."

-Ralph Waldo Emerson

FOREWORD

I Came...
I Saw...
I Heard The Stories...
Chods

The above platitude was hand-written on a <u>Pasta Bowl</u> tee shirt that was hanging behind the counter in the Rutgers Student Center. It is a saying that best represents the compiler of this book, in his job at that now-departed establishment, in the classroom and in life.

I have known Mike Chodroff for four years now and he is one of the brightest students who has ever taken my classes in Broadcast Journalism. He was always coming up with ideas, both wacky and wise, and looking for ways to implement them. He and his running mate, Adam Gaynor (a.k.a. The Senator), were always quick to develop storylines, camera angles, and plots which would better reflect the work and themselves. Their discussions about their in-class and out of class work quickly turned them into pseudo-legends in the Broadcast area.

So I was not surprised when Mike approached me with the idea for this book. As he waxed poetic about the hole that needed to be filled, that Rutgers students craved a better understanding of their own, unique, insular world, I could not help but agree. I knew of what he spoke.

I am a Rutgers College graduate (RC '79) and the absence of some definitive response to the questions all R.U. students have from first year to last day was never available. We all felt like the blind leading the blind trying to cut our way through the seemingly endless lines and bureaucracy in our attempts to make it through our four years on the banks. An informal information network told us when to sign up for meal plans, what courses were the best or worst, and what delights and defaults would meet us on the streets of New Brunswick.

In twenty years, nothing changed...until now. This book will be of great assistance to all Rutgers students who seek out the best of the university and its environs. Best of all, the opinions expressed in this tome come not from Old Queens or College Hall, but from the definitive Rutgers source: the students themselves.

After reading Mike's work, the tee shirt needs to be revised:

I Came...
I Saw...
I Heard The Stories...
I Wrote Them Down...

Steven A. Miller, January 1998

INTRODUCTION

So you want to know the ins and outs of Rutgers University? Or should I say the "unofficial bests and worsts". Well you certainly got your hands on the right publication to fulfill your curiosities.

I am a Rutgers graduate of '96 and spent my four years on the banks of the Old Raritan as many of you have, or are: studying, partying, working, learning, and just hanging around - and not necessarily in that order. That agenda is almost identical to what I do now in the "real world", and once again, not necessarily in that order.

My four years of college offered me a lot in terms of education both in and out of the classroom. More so out. I was pretty active at Rutgers, trying to make the most of my time meeting as many people as possible, not just for their friendships, but for their backgrounds and their knowledge. It was always important to me to keep an open mind in school, and still is today. It was always interesting to me to see what people's likes and dislikes were, and why it was that they felt and thought the way that they did.

That is probably the ultimate reason I came up with the idea for this book. And not just the idea, but the desire to completely forge ahead with it and make it as fun and thorough as possible for you - the students, alumni, affililiates of the university, or just curious onlookers. I wanted to put together what the likes and dislikes of the students were, in order to help eliminate the informal network that I had to go through to get these answers as an undergrad.

As is pointed out in the numerous disclaimers scattered throughout the beginning of this book, I put this together with a smirk. Yeah, I had a feeling that some of the information may be a little controversial, but I knew it was information that if excluded, would defeat the purpose of the book. I wanted to get the opinions of the students on the things that they encounter every single day - both bests and worsts. And keep in mind, every top ten list in this book is based on just that - opinions.

The way the lists came about, was after I got back the completed surveys, I carefully added up the amount of "votes" for each different subject. The surveys were phrased exactly how the topics in each chapter read, and had a blank line next to them. After tallying all of the information, I put together the top ten answers for each category.

Obviously, there are some feelings that are going to be uplifted when seeing this book, and others that may be hurt. But each topic should be viewed not just by the students, but by anyone affected by these lists as a potential source of information. Certainly there is no in-depth analysis as to why certain names and places appeared and others didn't. That kind of market research was not my intention. But perhaps the information can be used as a starting point for just that very thing. As a former student, and as a present entrepreneur, I know that criticism, both positive and negative is very important in achieving or maintaining any kind of success.

One final thing to note are the boxes full of comments at the end of each section. Any additional comments we found on the surveys, we wrote in, without censoring. I found them all very witty and strongly suggest that you take the time to read them.

Well, I hope you enjoy this book as much as I have enjoyed putting it together. And don't forget to read it with a smile!

The Rutgers Students Unofficial Guide to College

ACADEMICS

BEST MAJOR
Communication

207 & 208 4 Huntington St. (SCILS), CAC
(732) 932-8563

School of
Communication,
Information and
Library Studies

"Communication being chosen as the best major confirms what I have long known: that the faculty of the department is among the best at Rutgers in stimulating students to learn and assuring that the learning experience is as enjoyable as it is valuable.

"We all must use communication skills in our daily lives, no matter what our vocation, so the major is first and foremost relevant and useful. What can't you do with a major in communication? Not engineering or brain surgery, of course, nor accounting and opera singing. But you will have learned how to analyze the communication needs of an organization, how to find and organize info, how to collaborate and work on a team, and how to express yourself effectively. That makes you an ideal person for working in public relations, advertising, sales, human resources, not to mention mass media, book publishing, and yes, even the entertainment and sports industries. You could also get involved in government and politics. It's your choice!" - Todd Hunt, Dean of Dept. of Communication

2. Psychology
101 Tillet Hall, LC 445-4036

3. English
104 Murray Hall, CAC 932-7633

4. Engineering
Engineering Buildings - Busch Campus

5. Political Science
503 Hickman Hall, DC 932-9283

6. Business
39 Rockafeller Rd., LC 445-3600

7. Journalism & Mass Media
108 4 Huntington St. (SCILS), CAC 932-8567

8. Economics
202 New Jersey Hall, CAC 932-7482

9. Biology
A124 Nelson Biology Bldg., BC 445-5270

10. Pharmacy
103 Pharmacy Bldg., BC 445-2675

"Anything that can be done in 3 semesters" - Tanisha '99   "Sleep" - '01
"Beerology" - Dan   "any liberal art" - Keith '00   "C Major" - Tom
"Sheep molestation (this may only be a Cook major, I can't remember)" - '01
"For money or for easy classes? I guess Psychology is popular" - Megan '00
"Sexology" - Glenn '01   "Under Water Fire Prevention" - '00
"Undeclared!" - '00   "one that takes less than 6 years" - '98
"alcohol studies" - '99   "Marry rich" - Maria '99   "Major Dad" - '01

WORST MAJOR

Engineering

Different Disciplines of Engineering

Applied Sciences	Civil & Environmental
Industrial	Chemical & Biochemical
Biomedical	Ceramic and Materials
Electrical	Computer

2. Biology
A124 Nelson Biology Bldg., BC 445-5270

3. Mathematics
303 Hill Center, BC 445-2390

4. Pharmacy
103 Pharmacy Bldg., BC 445-2675

5. Chemistry
150 Wright/Reimann Laboratory, BC 445-2604

6. English
104 Murray Hall, CAC 932-7633

7. Biochemistry
A325 Nelson Biology Bldg., BC 445-3979

8. Psychology
101 Tillet Hall, LC 445-4036

9. Computer Science
390 Hill Center, BC 445-2001

10. Business
39 Rockafeller Rd., LC 445-3600

"Biology because it's so damn hard and you need 71 credits for it" - '98
"the study of pavement because you're too drunk to stand" - Dan
"anything requiring thinking" - '00   "Any Science or Math" - Keith '00
"Pharmacy - Hell now, will pay off later" - Jessica '01   "any -ology" - '99
"business anything - all those people are stressed" - Megan '00
"All are good because they attempt to better your education" - Melissa
"ones that involve work" - Ross '00   "a MAJOR headache from studying"

FAVORITE PROFESSOR

Prof. Daniel Ogilvie

Psychology Department
101 Tillet Hall, LC
(732) 445-4036

"Teaching is a very important part of being a professor and it's nice to be acknowledged when you are good at it. I work real hard on becoming comfortable in the classroom. It is absolutely essential to know the information cold. Once I get to that level, I can convey the information through stories that illustrate the concepts. Over the years, I have found that if I don't know the material, or if it's not up to date, then the lectures don't go as well as I'd like them to. If I do know the info, I can concentrate on the classroom community instead of having to be in my own mind."
- Professor Ogilvie

2. John Chapin
Communication Department

3. Maurice Charney
English Department

4. Joe Mancuso
Theater Arts Department

5. John Kenfield
Art History Department

6. Michael Welch
Administration of Justice Department

7. George Atwood
Psychology Department

8. Rob Doran
Mathematics Department

9. Steve Miller
Journalism & Mass Media Department

10. Todd Hunt
Communication Department

"If I could understand their names, I'd tell you" - '00
"I don't go to class" - '98   "the one who gives you an A" - '02
"Professor from *Gilligan's Island*" - '00   "a dead one" - '00
"one that speaks English properly" - Salvadore '99
"the one who never shows up" - '00   "the funny ones" - '98

LEAST FAVORITE PROFESSOR
Dr. Diana Martin

Biology Department

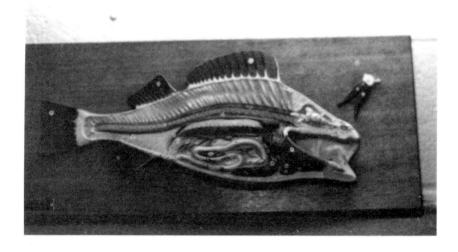

Quotations on teaching

"A poor surgeon hurts one person at a time. A poor teacher hurts [a whole classroom].   - Ernest Boyer

"What nobler employment, or more valuable to the state, than that of the man who instructs the rising generation?"   - Cicero

"The gift of teaching is a peculiar talent, and implies a need and a craving in the teacher himself."   - John Jay Chapman

2. Robert Karlin
Psychology Department

3. Henry Eng
Mathematics Department

4. William O'Neil
History Department

5. Douglass Blair
Economics Department

6. Cheryl Gooch
Communication Department

7. Rameshwar Agarwal
Chemistry Department

8. Jackson Toby
Sociology Department

9. Bert Brown
Psychology Department

10. Barbara Reed
Journalism & Mass Media Department

"2 years ago Rutgers invested in <u>Smart Technology</u> to enhance learning, now I ask, when will they invest in <u>smart professors</u> who can properly put these <u>smart tools</u> to use!?" - '99   "those that won't negotiate for an A" - '01 "Computer Science TA's" "all the professors who teach but you can't understand them because they barely speak English" - '98 "want me to list <u>all</u> of them?!!" - '00   "Any Expos prof." - '99 "ones that give me an F" - '00   "? (Too many choices)" - Christine '98 "The one from the creative writing course I dropped" - Leonardo "I hate everyone equally" - '01   "The one that can't speak English yet" - '01

BEST CLASSROOM
Scott 123
Scott Hall Lecture Room
College Avenue - Voorhees Mall

"It is in a really convenient location...five minutes from any dorm or off-campus house or apartment. Scott 123 is also a big enough room that if you get there early, you can get a seat in the front or hide in the back and read the paper or take a nap." - Jodi Varon, senior

2. Murray Hall Classrooms
College Avenue Campus

3. Lucy Stone Hall Auditorium
Livingston Campus

4. Beck Auditorium
Livingston Campus

5. Scott 135
College Avenue Campus

6. Scott Hall Classrooms
College Avenue Campus

7. Science and Engineering Resource Center (SERC)
Busch Campus

8. Voorhees 105
College Avenue Campus

9. Beck Hall Classrooms
Livingston Campus

10. Van Dyke 211
College Avenue Campus

"can any class really be that great?" - Rachel '98
"Binocular free vision of the professor"   "anything small" - '99
"The one with the most comfortable desk to have sex on" - '01
"outside class" - Eugene   "Someplace with leg room" - '00
"I don't go to class" - '98   "air conditioned in the summer" - '99
"Any auditorium" - Jeff '00   "Bedroom" - '98

WORST CLASSROOM
River Dorm Basements
Campbell, Frelinghuysen, and Hardenburg
George Street - CAC

"Hardenburgh Hall (is the worst classroom) because it is extremely noisy." - Nichole, sophomore

"Anything in the dorm basements because they smell like raw sewage." - Bonnie, junior

"Hardenburgh Hall B because it smells like cat litter." - senior

2. Beck Auditorium
Livingston Campus

3. Scott Hall Classrooms
College Avenue Campus

4. Scott 123
College Avenue Campus

5. Beck Hall Classrooms
Livingston Campus

6. Murray Hall Classrooms
College Avenue Campus

7. Lucy Stone Hall Auditorium
Livingston Campus

8. Taylor Road Building
Busch Campus

9. (Tie) Hickman Hall Classrooms / Milledoler 100
Douglass Campus / College Avenue Campus

10. Physics Lecture Hall
Busch Campus

"Any classroom in Lucy Stone Hall - the heat's on in the summer and the air's on in the winter" - Skeeter   "any with those little flip desks" - Faithe '98
"Hot ones" - '99   "500 student lectures"   "anywhere on Livingston" - '99
"Cinema room, top floor Murray Hall" - no ventilation" - Jen '98
"EN-B120, nobody can figure out how to use the electric moving blackboards" - '99
"any room in Beck - I feel like I'm in solitary confinement because there are no windows!" - Nicole '01   "one's that compete in size with Giants Stadium"
"Voorhees 105 - it's a cold, dark, mean room" - Jen '00   "Small rooms in Scott Hall"

BEST PLACE TO STUDY

Alexander Library
College Avenue - CAC
(732) 932-7851

Circulation Desk	General Collections	Undergrad Reading Room
Mon-Thurs	Mon-Thurs	Mon-Thurs
9:00am-11:00pm	8:00am-12:00am	8:00am-1:00am
Friday	Friday	Friday
9:00am-8:30pm	8:00am-9:00pm	8:00am-9:00pm
Saturday	Saturday	Saturday
10:30am-7:30pm	10:00am-8:00pm	10:00am-8:00pm
Sunday	Sunday	Sunday
12:30pm-11:00pm	NOON-12:00am	NOON-1:00am

2. In your room

3. At home

4. Rutgers Student Center

5. Dorm hallway lounge

6. Dorm quiet study lounge

7. Art History Library

8. Au Bon Pain

9. Kilmer Library

10. Science and Engineering Resource Center (SERC)

"anywhere you can hide from friends" - Amy '00   "The Roost" - Lori '96
"Rutgers Football Stadium" - '00   "In the class before the test" - Kairida '99
"at good looking girls place" - Eugene   "Tunnels in New Gibbons" - '00
"Late Night Study @ Brower for Finals" - Katie '99   "Who studies?" - '00
"My dreams"   "Kilmer (no one's ever there), Alexander is too social" - Chad '00
"Hill Center - top is absolutely silent" - Tim '01   "Haven't found it yet" - '99
"Douglass Library Reference Room - no one is ever there, you have a large table
  all to yourself with gigantic windows and you have computers next to you, so
  you can check e-mail when you are frustrated or procrastinating" - Lana '99
"Church during finals" - Carolina '99   "in the privacy of your own room" - '00
"How the hell would I know!" - '00   "International Room - BSC" - '00
"in those big, comfortable leather chairs in Alexander Library" - '98

BEST WAY TO CHEAT

Don't Cheat!

"Academic freedom is a fundamental right in any institution of higher learning. Honesty and integrity are necessary preconditions of this freedom. Academic integrity requires that all academic work be wholly the product of an identified individual or individuals... Ethical conduct is the obligation of every member of the University community, and breaches of academic integrity constitute serious offenses...

"Students must assume responsibility for maintaining honesty in all work submitted for credit and in any other work designated by the instructor of the course. Students are also expected to report incidents of academic dishonesty to the instructor or dean of the instructional unit."

Rutgers University, New Brunswick Campus Policy on Academic Integrity

2. Copy someone next to you

3. Programmable Calculator

4. Cheat Sheet

5. Sit next to friends

6. Get a copy of the test

7. Sleep with the professor

8. Write the answers on the desk

9. Write the answers on hat brim

10. Have someone else take the test for you

"Good students don't cheat - they verify" - '01   "carve into a pencil" - '00
"for multiple choice tests - assign a letter to the desk corners and E is the middle"
"don't cheat...bullshit" - '98   "hold professor hostage until you get an A" - '99
"have a piece of paper secretly placed on the floor then pretend to keep dropping
  things so you can look at it" - '00   "it is not cheating unless you get caught" - '99
"Find the nearest Asian kid" - '00   "take Communication...you don't need to"
"answers written on shoe" - '00   "Come on now - that's wrong!" - '99
"sleep with professor and steal answers from his briefcase (really happened)" - '98
"with one of her friends" - '98   "blow your nose once for a, twice for b..." - '96
"it's easy - you can write things anywhere from your body parts to the desk you sit
  at...or just ask your classroom buddy for the answers! I never tried cheating
  though..." - '00   "with someone hot" - '01   "Whatever works" - '99
"Write down notes on piece of paper, wear overalls and tape the notes inside of the
  front bib so when you lean over you can look down and see the answers. Works
  everytime" - '98   "Foot taps - one tap is a, two taps is b..." - '99   "TI-82" - '00
"Give your professor a tie with the answers on it. They'll wear it because they
  need new clothes" - '01   "never give away my secrets" - '99   "Band aids"
"sleep with the professor. Those old men are good, too! Even the women!" - '99

The Rutgers Students Unofficial Guide to College

Life in the dorms

BEST DORM
Clothier Hall

Corner of George Street and Bishop Place - CAC
Typically - all Freshman Dorm

"We used to call Clothier 'the Zoo'. We used to party all the time and get away with just about everything. I made a lot of good friends there. Most everyone I know, I met in Clothier. Living there definately effected my G.P.A.!"
- Christian Daglieri, senior

2. University Center at Easton Avenue
College Avenue Campus

3. Hardenburgh Hall
College Avenue Campus

4. Campbell Hall
College Avenue Campus

5. McCormick Suite
Busch Campus

6. (Tie) Tinsley Hall / Brett Hall
College Avenue Campus

7. Livingston Quads
Livingston Campus

8. Allen Hall
Busch Campus

9. Frelinghuysen Hall
College Avenue Campus

10. Mattia Hall
Busch Campus

"Frelinghuysen - good TV reception" - Steven '98
"none - Frats all the way" - '95   "Home" - '99
"Allen - they have automatic toilets" - Leah '01

WORST DORM

Livingston Quads

Corner of Road 3 and Avenue E
Livingston Campus

"The Quads are definately the worst dorms, because they are the most dangerous. One time, at 2:00am, a friend and I were chased by ten big guys in the tunnels underneath the dorms. I thought I was going to be raped or killed. We probably should have reported it to the Rutgers police but we were too scared. We had a lot of fun in the dorm, but it was just really dangerous because of the connecting tunnels."

- Becky, senior

2. Davidson Hall
Busch Campus

3. Demarest Hall
College Avenue Campus

4. Clothier Hall
College Avenue Campus

5. Brett Hall
College Avenue Campus

6. Stonier Hall
College Avenue Campus

7. Towers
Livingston Campus

8. Campbell Hall
College Avenue Campus

9. Hegeman Hall
College Avenue Campus

10. New Gibbons
Douglass Campus

"Davidson Barracks" - Veronique '00   "Take your pick" - '98
"Brett - the most socially retarded people live there" - '99
"The Quadjects" - '99   "Stonier - no socialization" - '99
"Anything not on College Ave" - Natalie '98   "hard to decide"

BEST THING ABOUT YOUR ROOM

Lots of space

"We have a bar, a sofa bed for any girls that want to stay over, and all the room for one guy to play Sega while ten guys stand around and watch. We also have a work out bench in the closet that can be pulled out and used in the room. Big rooms give us the ability to never have to leave the room. If there was a bathroom in it, it would be perfect."

- Joseph Puzzo and Doug Walsh, juniors

2. The bed

3. My roommate

4. The windows

5. The view

6. The way it is decorated

7. It's a single

8. Has a big closet

9. (Tie) Air conditioning / The location

10. Has carpeting

"It's the bomb! Everything's awesome" - Lauren '99   "My bong" - '00
"It's not forever..."   "My flannel sheets" - '01   "My bar" - '00
"I live off campus" - Renee '99   "many condoms" - Barron '98
"Highlighter on walls that you can only see with the blacklight on" - '98
"not being in it" - '00   "No bars on the windows" - Mary '96
"my quotes on the wall" - Jean '01   "Dart board" - Bob '00
"No strange stains on the carpet like last year (strange stains on the
ceiling instead) - '00   "It's mine and mine alone" - '99
"mirror on the ceiling" - Kevin '98   "Hugging Pillow" - '01
"the mess" - Gil '99   "the freedom that comes with it" - Ianna '01
"can study there"   "feels like home" - Limin '99   "video camera" - '96

WORST THING ABOUT YOUR ROOM

Not enough space

"Because we live in a triple it is always cramped. There are only two closets for three people and there are three sets of furniture, half of which are messed up. Also, there is someone always in the room. You have to make sure it is okay with two people to have friends in the room, who barely fit anyway."

- Meghan Flanagan, freshman

2. My roommate

3. Bugs

4. Poor lighting

5. Dirty/Messy

6. Cinderblock walls

7. Smells funky

8. Too hot

9. Asbetos ceiling

10. The tacky curtains

"looks like a mental institution" - '00   "Too many distractions" - '01
"living by the door and drunk people without slash cards banging on window
to let them in" - '99   "Fire Martials come by at free will" - '00   "Flies" - '00
"Curtains are 70's rejects" - Stephanie '00   "Have to clean bathroom" - '01
"all the rooms are beige" - Tim '01   "the fridge doesn't hold all the beer"
"No Jacuzzi" - '98   "roommate's sweater-vests" - '98   "Thin walls" - '98
"Paint chips falling from the ceiling" - Jack '00   "It's a dorm room" - Laura '00
"Tacky furniture came with it" - Jen '98   "shades don't block sunrise" - '00
"My books" - '01   "No hammock" - Melissa '98   "Alarm clock" - Rob '99
"My roommates' constant scaring away influx of women"   "Firedrills" - '99
"no cable TV" - Rich '00   "It is one square foot bigger than a closet" - Mario
"In it, alone every weekend with my Organic book on my squeaky ass bed"
"smells like moth balls from roommate" - '01   "no beer kegs" - '00

BEST THING ABOUT YOUR ROOMMATE
Someone to talk to / complain to

"I was put in a triple freshman year with complete strangers. Now, four years later they are my two best friends. Whenever I need someone, no matter how busy they are, they always find time for me."
- Christine Cerniglia, senior

2. Never around

3. Best friends

4. Cool, easy going, & laid back

5. Very compatible

6. Nice & polite

7. Someone to hang out with

8. Funny

9. Considerate & caring

10. They're quiet

"cool talks before bed and take-out food" - '98   "Not a druggie"
"We're both Gemini" - Andrea '00   "he makes me look good" - '99
"we know when to leave each other alone" - '00   "Not a jerk" - '01
"her clothes" - '00   "Good looking girls are his friends" - Dave '99
"lets me listen while having sex" - '00   "She's mad cool" - '00
"lied to boys for me, (not to mention parents) - '98   "Musical talent"
"always buys beer" - '01   "she's my sister" - '98   "love and support"
"he paid the phone bills on time" - '00   "Disney/Kermit fanatic" - '01
"big and strong" - '01   "you don't have to live with them forever"
"has become family" - Nicoletta '99   "my roommate is a saint" - '01
"keeps me awake when I need to study" - '00   "CD player" - '00
"she makes my bed" - Bonnie '99   "puts up with me" - Melissa '00

WORST THING ABOUT YOUR ROOMMATE

Messy / Slob

Quotations on tidiness

"He who has no taste for order, will be often wrong in his judgement, and seldom considerate or conscientious in his actions."
- John Casper Lavater

"So great is the effect of cleanliness upon man, that it extends even to his moral character. Virtue never dwelt long with filth; nor do I believe there ever was a person scrupulously attentive to cleanliness who was a consummate villain." - Count Benjamin Thomas Rumford

2. Smells funny

3. No privacy (in the room too much)

4. Nothing

5. Annoying & irritating

6. Their girlfriend/boyfriend

7. Sleeps too much

8. Not around enough

9. Talks too much

10. Snores

"My roommate was in a cult (don't print my name if you print this one)"
"bad pornos" - '00   "she plays with her belly button" - '00   "a grub"
"he smells like an old person" - '01   "she slept with my boyfriend" - '99
"walks around naked" - '98   "convinces me not to go to class" - Lanie '00
"He's a nice guy, I can't think of anything" - Leonardo   "thinks I'm a loser" - '00
"she jumps up on my bed at 7am when I don't have morning classes" - Rita '00
"he is more endowed than I am" - '01   "she sleeps sitting upright" - '00
"he makes me leave when he has sex" - Jeff '00   "Eats Gerber baby food" - '98
"sometimes she doesn't have weed" - '00   "Keeps the lights on at night" - '01
"talks through every movie" - Danielle '00   "insomniac with mood swing" - '01
"gets laid more than me" - '00   "She lets the alarm go off for ions" - '00
"always drunk" - '98   "they know too much" - '01   "No Friday classes (Grr...)"
"I think she's going to kill me" - '01   "too damn materialistic" - '01
"has bad timing"   "He's an asshole" - '01   "Sloppy hook-ups" - '99
"has influence on me" - Bobby '98   "sleeps with eyes open" - '99   "sheds hair"

BEST ROOMMATE PRANK

See list on next page

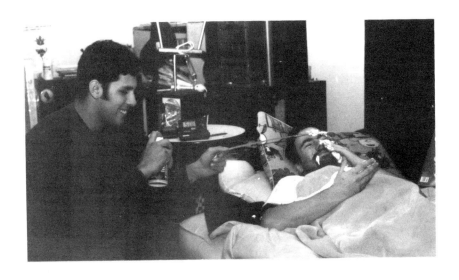

"It is difficult to say who do you the most mischief, enemies with the worst intentions, or friends with the best." - Edward Lytton-Bulwer

"Beating him in his sleep" "Stuffing garbage under door"
"Penny locking the door during finals" "Toothpaste in shoes"
"Tell them nasty things that people think about them but don't
 let them know who said it" "Pretend to be having sex"
"Hiding his mattress" "Frozen underwear" "Toilet wars"
"Red hots in cereal" "Taking towel while in the shower"
"Wedgies" "Taking pictures of them while they sleep"
"Ejaculate in his shampoo" "Toenail clippings everywhere"
"Sharpen knives in front of her and how crazy you are"
"Turn off the lights while they're pooping" "Tie the door shut"
"Put shoe on ceiling with crazy glue" "Water/ice in bed"
"Lean a garbage can full of water against the door and knock"
"Plastic spiders in soapdish" "Wear their favorite outfit"
"Set alarm for 8am at maximum blast" "Reading his diary"
"Tell 'em you got kicked out of RU and start moving stuff out"
"Steal keys" "Jump out of the closet and scare them"
"Changing his computer settings" "Sand in the vasoline"
"Hiding her medication" "Wipe boogars on their desk"
"Feces in pillow case" "Shave his leg while he is sleeping"
"Turn dresser upside down and put everything back on top"
"Condoms on doorknob" "Putting all his stuff in the lounge"
"Pretend to be deaf" "Steal car when she has to go to work"
"Tell her that you're pregnant" "Hide computer keyboard"
"Leave your alarm on when you go home for the weekend"
"De-register them" "Shaving cream in hand when sleeping"
"Locking them out after they shower" "Setting him on fire"
"Nair in hair stuff" "Cellophane over toilet bowl" "Kill him"
"Hit on all the girls he meets" "Send AA recruitment letter"

BEST RULE TO BREAK
Alcohol Policy

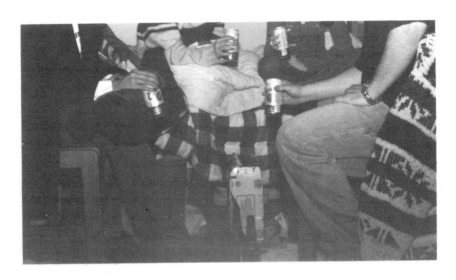

"Serving and/or consumption of alcoholic beverages on university property, which includes your room or apartment, must fully comply with all university regulations as well as local, state, and federal laws and regulations."

Rutgers University Housing Policy

2. No noise during quiet hours

3. No pot smoking

4. No smoking in the room or lounge

5. No parties

6. No burning candles

7. No burning incense

8. No microwaves

9. No pets

10. No halogen lamps

"running with scissors" - '00   "no extension cords" - Melissa '99
"the implied rule that you shouldn't hook up with somebody on your
 floor, but the floor that sleeps together, stays together and if you can't
 keep it in your pants, keep it in the hall" - '99   "Vandalism" - '01
"Showering in the opposite sex's bathroom with the opposite sex" - '01
"Ripping rules off wall" - Christine '98   "Public lewdness" - Glenn '01
"lynch the preceptor that has a thing for busting you" - '01   "no fish"
"Stay in during fire alarm" - Mike '99   "lounge furniture theft" - '00
"question authority" - '01   "Having guys sleep over all the time" - '00
"drinking and smoking when the RA is with us" - '99   "No kegs" - '99

The Rutgers Students Unofficial Guide to College

Living off
Campus

BEST STREET TO LIVE ON
Easton Avenue

"Living on Easton Avenue, you can find the best bars, places to eat, and places to relax and have a cup of coffee or some ice-cream. It is also close to the classrooms, the student center, and the train station."
- Kristy Gillio, senior

2. Stone St.

3. Guilden St.

4. Senior St.

5. Mine St.

6. Sicard St.

7. Prosper St.

8. Hamilton Ave.

9. (Tie) College Ave. / Richardson St.

10. Ray St.

"Sicard Street - runs through everything" - '99
"Central Avenue - great parking all the time" - Melissa '98
"Richardson - near the library, nice area, and low crime"
"any street within four blocks of College Avenue" - '99
"Guilden Street - lots of parties" - Francis '99
"any off Route 18" - Amritha '00   "Stone & High - the names"
"Senior St. - perfect place for beer, pizza, gyros, and weed"

WORST STREET TO LIVE ON
George Street

"Let's just put it this way, last year I made the silly mistake of living on George Street and it pretty much ruined my whole social life. Because it was so unsafe to walk around at night, let alone stand near the window, I never went out. I was counting the days until my lease was up."

- Amy, graduate student

2. Louis St.

3. Easton Ave.

4. Hamilton Ave.

5. Somerset St.

6. Plum St.

7. Commercial Ave.

8. Livingston Ave.

9. Guilden St.

10. Delafield St.

"Throop Ave. (the street where everyone in New Brunswick
  gets shot at)" - '98   "George Street - the ghetto area" - Mario
"Hamilton St. - too many crackhouses"   "Frat row" - Ani '99
"Anywhere in downtown New Brunswick" - Salvadore '99
"Anything past Easton Ave." - '99   "any w/ a lot of old residents"
"Hamilton - I woke up to the sounds of jackhammers @ 6-7 am
  everyday for 3 months" - '98   "any far from College Ave" - '00

BEST LEASE POLICY TO BREAK
No Parties

Taken from a standard lease...

Clause 11. Violating Laws and Causing Disturbances

Tenant is entitled to quiet enjoyment of the premises. Tenant and guests or
invitees will not use the premises or adjacent areas in such a way as to: (1)
violate any law or ordinance, including laws prohibiting the use, possession or
sale of illegal drugs; (2) commit waste (severe property damage); or (3) create
a nuisance by annoying, disturbing, inconveniencing or interfering with the
quiet enjoyment and peace and quiet of any other tenant or nearby resident.

2. No Pets

3. Number of tenants allowed

4. No drinking or having kegs

5. Paying rent on time

6. No bedroom in attic or basement

7. No violating noise ordinance

8. No smoking in the house

9. No subletting

10. No going out on the roof

"illegal sweatshop in the basement" - Bobby '98
"no puffin' in the house (whatever!)"   "sex on the roof" - '00
"The one about knocking down walls" - Clint '95
"flushing tampons down the toilet" - Renee '00   "no giraffes"
"people in attic" - Sheila '00   "paying garbage fines" - '97
"reporting damage as a result of a great party" - Stacey '99
"no beer pong on front porch" - Beth '99   "no BBQs" - '98
"uh...I don't have a lease" - Sal '99   "leaving 2 months early"

FINISH THIS SENTENCE:

MY LANDLORD/ LANDLADY IS...

Non-existent / Never around

"I can't even think of a reason why he shows up. He doesn't even show up for rent. If we want something fixed we have to do it ourselves. The funniest thing is that he told us the other day that he is tired of coming around to fix things. Last time he was here and told us the same thing was five months ago."
- Lior, freshman

2. an asshole

3. a bitch

4. cheap

5. hot/cute

6. (Tie) fat / a bastard

7. nice/good

8. cool

9. lazy

10. a thief/rip-off

"a money hungry bitch!"   "a dominatrix"   "a dirty, stingy, old bastard"
"horrible. Doesn't get anything done. Sees my Janice Joplin poster and tells
me about his pot smoking days and not being quite done with them yet"
"on crack"   "a lazy prick who I sued"   "a porn star!"   "a devil worshipper"
"really blind not to see a bong through the window"   "a loose cannon"
"a fucking scumbag con-artist"   "sexually aroused by cement"   "not nice"
"a beligerant old fart, an overly pretentious bastard, a worthless steaming
pile of cow dung! Figuratively speaking"   "spankariffic!"   "from hell"
"a potsmoking, coke snorting, cheap asshole"   "a retarded little fat man"
"actually a great guy. He fixes everything and is pretty cool with everything"
"hemorraging from her ears. I really don't know why"   "a child molester"
"a whore who trades sex for rent"   "a slumlord"   "a large spider"
"rich by now"   "a mob boss"   "cranky"   "the owner of fucked up teeth"
"we have one? I never see him except to collect rent"   "sleeping with me"
"an asshole who likes to cheat innocent college kids"   "missing in action"

The Rutgers Students Unofficial Guide to College

FOOD

BEST BROWER MEAL

Mexican Cantina

"Mexican Cantina is definately the best meal because it leaves your body so much faster than any other food. Just like Taco Bell, grade D...but edible. I like having the ability to put together my own food and it just damn tastes good!"
- Alex Barenbaum, senior

2. Mashed potatoes

3. Hot turkey

4. Pasta

5. Thanksgiving meal

6. Chicken tenderloins

7. Grilled cheese

8. Salad bar

9. Subs

10. Macaroni and cheese

"Four day customized meatloaf with raisins" - Brian '99   "Bleah!!" - '99
"Water & Ice"   "Yuck, who wants to eat dining hall food" - Nichole '00
"There is one?" - '99   "We don't use favorable adjectives to describe
 Brower meals" - Rachel '00   "Are you kidding me!" - '00
"Trick question" - '01   "All Brower food causes the shits" - Mike '98
"The chocolate chip cookies" - Erin '00   "Strictly Busch, man" - '01
"They have a lot of cockroaches - They force students to eat there.
 It is a conspiracy!" - '99   "Still waiting for that one" - '01
"They are all terrible - but best is one that in not still alive" - '99

BEST RESTAURANT
Old Man Rafferty's
106 Albany Street - New Brunswick
(732) 846-6153

"We are very flattered and happy about being chosen as the best restaurant. It shows that all the hard work that we put in pays off and is appreciated.

"Location and affordability are definately key as being important to students and we have both. At the same time, if someone wants to do something nicer for a meal or take someone out on a date, this is also the place to come. We get a lot of students, alumni, families and business people. Students love bringing their parents here. We thank everyone very much for their patronage and definately enjoy the students here. It wouldn't be the same without them." - Erica Schor, manager

2. Stuff Yer Face
49 Easton Ave. New Brunswick 247-1727

3. Church Street Trattoria
94 Church St. New Brunswick 828-4355

4. Teresa's Pizzetta Cafe
48 Easton Ave. New Brunswick 545-3737

5. Neubie's
120 Somerset St. New Brunswick 846-0999

6. Tumulty's
361 George St. New Brunswick 545-6205

7. (Tie) Marita's Cantina / The Round Grill
Ferren Deck Mall 247-3840 / Ferren Deck Mall 828-3337

8. (Tie) Harvest Moon / Sapparo
392 George St. 249-6666 / 375 George St. 828-3888

9. Clyde's
55 Paterson Ave. New Brunswick 846-6521

10. The Old Bay
61-63 Church St. New Brunswick 246-3111

"N/A - I eat Kosher" - junior   "Downstairs Fridge"
"Too many good choices" - sophomore   "Brower" - Leo
"I'll go any place as long as the servers are good" - '98

BEST PIZZA
Skinny Vinnie's
60 Sicard Street - New Brunswick
(732) 545-6671

"We are delighted that the students picked us as the best pizza on campus. I think the quality comes from over 18 years of experience. Thank you very much and we hope that everybody comes in to try our pizza." - Manny, manager

"One of my fondest memories of Rutgers was living right across the street from Skinny Vinnie's. Late night studying and partying would not have been the same if I wasn't so close to the best pizza on campus. Damn, it was good." - Jason Marino

2. Pizza City
145 Easton Ave. New Brunswick 937-9597

3. PJ.'s Grill and Pizza
166 Easton Ave. New Brunswick 249-2919

4. Pizza Hut
78 Albany St. New Brunswick 246-4240

5. La Familia
160 Easton Ave. New Brunswick 937-9500

6. Gerlanda's Pizza Cafe
Rutgers Student Center - CAC 846-9375

7. Marco's
34 Easton Ave. New Brunswick 545-3800

8. Tata's
208 Hamilton St. New Brunswick 846-6232

9. Domino's
1677 Route 27 Edison 572-1441

10. Lanova Italian Kitchen
142 Easton Ave. New Brunswick 828-1128

"Early in the night - Skinny Vinnie's / after bars - Pizza City at $1.00 a slice" - Heather '98   "Cold" - James '99
"Depends on how drunk you are" - '98   "Shroom pie" - '00

BEST CHINESE FOOD
Noodle Gourmet
43 Easton Avenue - New Brunswick
(732) 828-8188

"I am so happy that the students like my food. They chose me so I am going to keep doing my best to get even better for the students. I hope that the students keep coming back and choose me as the best for next year. The secret to us being so good is that I am here all the time to keep my eyes on my kitchen and my business. I watch to guarantee that we work hard to ensure quality food, and according to the students, I guess we do." - Ken, owner

"Every Sunday night my friends and I order take out from Noodle Gourmet and we eat it in the dorm lounge. It is always fresh and hot." - sophomore

"I come here a lot because the food is really good and inexpensive. My favorite dishes are Hong Kong style Beef Chow Mein and Gourmet Chow Udon" - Mee Sun Choi, sophomore

2. Szechwan Gourmet
3 Livingston Ave. New Brunswick 846-7878

3. Szechwan Express
Rutgers Student Center - CAC 249-8818

4. Kin's Restaurant
174 Easton Ave. New Brunswick 418-7139

5. Hong Kong Kitchen
90 Remsen Ave. New Brunswick 249-9888

6. Lin's Garden
569 Somerset St. Franklin 246-8820

7. Hunan East
1167 Route 27 Highland Park 572-5293

8. Gold Coin
517 Raritan Ave. Highland Park 572-5293

9. Golden East Garden
Route 18 Mid State Mall East Brunswick 257-3737

List of Chinese food that students wrote as their favorite

Beef Chow Fun	Water Chestnuts	Kung-Po Chicken
Chicken w/ Broccoli	Roast Pork Lo Mein	Pineapple Chicken
Orange Beef	Sweet & Sour Chicken	Rice w/ soy sauce
Egg Roll	Beef Fried Rice	Chicken Chow Mein
Wonton Soup	General Tso's Chicken	Brocolli w/ garlic
Sesame Chicken	Beef w/ snow peas	Egg Foo Young

BEST COFFEE
Starbucks Coffee
391 George Street - New Brunswick
(732) 418-9060

"We have always had a good rapport with the students. They love coming here and all of them are so nice and friendly. I'm glad they feel they can come in here to relax and study. In terms of this company, Starbucks is very supportive of their employees. They also support a lot of great social programs. For example, they run a literary program that helps teach people to read."
- Shannon, manager

2. Dunkin Donuts
Cook Campus Center 932-5079 / Livingston Student Center 445-4736

3. Au Bon Pain
126 College Ave. New Brunswick 873-9845

4. Cafe 52
52 Easton Ave. New Brunswick 249-1900

5. Gerlanda's Pizza Cafe
Rutgers Student Center - CAC 846-9375

6. Grease Trucks
Grease Truck parking lot - across from Scott Hall - CAC

7. Brew Ha-Ha's
Douglass College Center - DC 932-9775

8. (Tie) Mabel's / Neubies
Douglass College Center 932-1852 / 120 Somerset St. 846-0999

9. Thomas Sweet
55 Easton Ave. New Brunswick 828-3855

10. (Tie) Theresa's / Easton Grill & Bagel Co.
48 Easton Ave. 545-3737 / 194 Easton Ave. 296-1666

"Isn't coffee an illegal substance in this dorm?" - '01
"Super Java Fuel" - '98   "Instant" - Christina '00
"I'm probably the only college student that does not like
  coffee, so none" - Rachel '98   "Strong & Black" - '00
"Vending machine in the Hill Center basement" - '99

BEST MIDDLE EASTERN FOOD
Grease Trucks

Grease Truck Parking Lot - Across from Scott Hall
College Avenue

"The grease truck food is not as good as it was in Israel, but it is a good runner-up in terms of food prepared here in America. Where else can you go when you have a craving for falafel and hotsauce at 2:00 in the morning?"
- Jessica Wohl, senior

2. Jimmy's Grille Specialite
104 Easton Ave. New Brunswick 418-9600

3. Evelyn's Restaurant
45 Easton Ave. New Brunswick 246-8792

4. R.U. Hungry
Grease Truck parking lot - CAC

5. Mr. C's
Grease Truck parking lot - CAC

6. Sunrise
Grease Truck parking lot - CAC

7. The Round Grill
Ferren Deck Mall New Brunswick 828-3337

8. Campus Deli
82 Senior St. New Brunswick 828-4011

9. (Tie) Road Deli / Jordan's
Grease Truck parking lot - CAC

10. (Tie) Giovanelli's / P.J.'s Grill and Pizza
60 Easton Ave 220-1220 / 166 Easton Ave. 249-2919

List of Middle Eastern food that students wrote as their favorite

Falafel	Baklava	Babaghanouge	Tabouli
Somosas	Homous	Spinach Pie	Shish kebob
Gyro	Fat Cat	Grape leaves stuffed with rice	

BEST PLACE TO GRAB A QUICK MEAL

Grease Trucks

Grease Truck Parking Lot - Across from Scott Hall
College Avenue

"The grease trucks could be done and should be done every single night. It is amazing how they all remember your name from years ago. Grease trucks are a way of life and you don't feel like your day is complete if you haven't grabbed a bite to eat from them."

- Gil Lieblich, junior

2. Student Center
Rutgers, Busch, Cook, Douglass, Livingston

3. Wendy's
Rutgers Student Center / Busch Student Center

4. Jimmy's Grille Specialite
104 Easton Ave. New Brunswick 418-9600

5. (Tie) Au Bon Pain / P.J.'s Grill and Pizza
126 College Ave. 873-9845 / 166 Easton Ave. 249-2919

6. McDonald's
Ferren Deck Mall New Brunswick 828-5208

7. Dining Hall
Brower, Busch, Cooper, Davidson, Neilson, Tillett

8. R.U. Hungry
Grease Truck parking lot - CAC

9. Gerlanda's Pizza Cafe
Rutgers Student Center - CAC 846-9375

10. (Tie) Stuff Yer Face / Skinny Vinnie's
49 Easton Ave. 247-1727 / 60 Sicard St. 545-6671

"All my meals take time" - '99   "Wendy's - Yeah! Frosties!"
"Deiner Park" - '98 "Mom's house (10 minutes away)" - Awi
"Who has time to eat?" - '01   "My fridge" - Lauren '98
"Grease truck, if you want to deal with minor heart attacks
immediately following your meal." - Andy '99   "Dumpster"

NJ Monthly's "Best Casual Italian Food"

- August, 1997

gourmet pizza

fresh pasta

homemade desserts

cappucino • espresso

Under New Ownership
Same Great Food - Large Portions
Expanded Menu

we do parties & catering

mon-thurs: 11:30 am - 10 pm
fri-sat: 11:30 am - 11 pm
sun: 2 pm - 10 pm
We Validate Parking - Handicapable Accessible

Now Available outdoor dining May - Sept

94 church street • new brunswick
828-4355

3 Livingston Ave., New Brunswick
846-7878

Mon-Fri • 11:30am - 2:00am
Sat & Sun • Noon - 2:00am

"★★★★ from NY Daily News"

"A taste of Chinatown...Szechwan Gourmet offers a massive menu well worth studying." - *The Home News & Tribune*

FREE DELIVERY TO ALL CAMPUSES	10% OFF Eat-In Only with valid Student I.D.

For the best quality food and the best price value...listen to the critics

Social Life at College

WHAT DO YOU DO IN YOUR FREE TIME?

Sleep

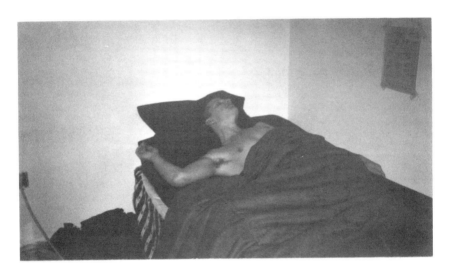

"You get no time to yourself when in college, so if you should be lucky enough to have a moment or two to call your own, use it wisely. My suggestion is take a nap!"
- Laura, freshman

2. Have sex

3. Drink

4. Hang out with friends

5. (Tie) Smoke pot / Watch TV

6. Play various sports

7. Masturbate

8. Study

9. Go to the gym or do exercise

10. Read

"drink, sex, video games, football, sex" - John '99   "procrastinate" - '00
"Atari and Alcohol" - '98   "Drink a few and smoke a bunch" - Rob '98
"Figure out why New Brunswick has no functional video store" - '00
"Complain" - Jared '00   "recover from Brower Commons food" - '98
"anything that has nothing to do with school" - Andrew '99
"bother my roommate" - '00   "have sex / write poetry" - '99
"Have a six pack, smoke a doob, pop in *The Shining*" - '01
"Laugh my ass off!" - Matt '00   "What free time?" - '98   "Just do it" - '99
"Watch Family Feud and make cookies at 1:00 am" - Suchi '98
"calculate my potential GPA" - '99   "play beer games" - Kevin '98
"worry about what I am going to do with a degree in English Lit." - '99

BEST PLACE TO MEET GIRLS

In Class

"Now that I am graduating, I guess I can give away my warning to girls...when a guy asks you if you want to study for an exam, it actually means that he wants to get into your bedroom. Man, I'm gonna miss going to class." - senior, anonymous

2. At the bars

3. In the dorms

4. At a frat party

5. On Douglass

6. In the girls bathroom

7. At the library

8. At a house party

9. In the dining halls

10. At the student centers

"Voorhees Mall in Spring" - Jeff '00   "College, itself" - '00
"Normal life activities. You can't go looking for girls, good
things happen as your life progresses. There is also a greater
chance you will have similar interests this way" - Steven '99
"Anywhere they are" - Brian '99   "in a convent" - Eric '98
"Parties (if alcohol is involved, you're more likely to approach
people...)" - Oliver '99   "If you find out, tell me" - Mike '98
"There's no particular place to meet girls" - Skeeter '98

BEST PLACE TO MEET GUYS
At bars

"The best place to meet guys is in the bar because when you are drunk, you have no inhibitions. During the week you schlep to class and don't get dressed up. Going to the bars to hang out and meet people is not like second period in Murray where you show up in your pajamas."
- Kristina Kersey, senior

2. In class

3. At a frat party

4. At the gym

5. In the dorms

6. At a house party

7. In the dining halls

8. At the library

9. At a sporting event

10. In the boys bathroom

"I haven't found it yet" - '98   "Student Center arcade room"
"Nice guys = class / Bad boys = bars" - Kristen '98
"in class - one of the few places most RU students are
 sober" - Nicole '01   "Downtown New Brunswick" - Sarah '00
"Ballroom Dancing Class - Seriously!" - Sophie '99
"Security shuttle" - Jessica '99   "Demarest Hall" - Gary '00

BEST CLUB/ ORGANIZATION TO JOIN
Residence Hall Presidents Council (RHPC)

Contact: Office of Residence Life : Bishop House - (732) 932-7209
Richardson Community Center - (732) 445- 4399

"This surprising honor is an attribute to how the organization has grown over the last few years. The student body has responded and RHPC will continue to fulfill their need as the best organization to join. What makes us so great is that the connection we have with the students in personal. It is in the halls, a comfortable setting in which to operate. The students don't have problems talking with us because we are one large family."
- Chuck Berninger, President

"Our purpose is to create a positive atmosphere in the halls. We do this through various activities that bring all the students in the dorms together. Harmony Day and the annual cruise are some highlights." - Jason Redd, V.P

2. Rutgers Union for Gay and Bisexual Men (RUGBI)
Dept. of Health Education Hurtado Health Center - Attn. RUGBI

3. The Daily Targum
932-7051

4. Bisexual, Gay, Lesbian Alliance of RU (BIGLARU)
932-7501

5. Marching Band
445-2480

6. (Tie) RU Outdoors Club (RUOC) / WRSU 88.7 FM
932-1580 / 932-7800

7. (Tie) Rutgers College Program Council (RCPC) / Rutgers College Governing Association (RCGA)
932-7213 / 932-6978

8. Public Relations Student Society of America (PRSSA)
932-7914

9. N.J. Interest Research Group Student Chapters (NJPIRG)
932-7131

10. (Tie) Children's AIDS Network (CAN) / New Student Orientation (NSO)
932-9327 / 932-8384

"NORML (National Organization for the Reform of Marijuana Laws)" - '00
"Mile High Club" - Maurice '99   "RU Having Sex" - '98   "As if I have time"
"Student Advisors, you get to move in early and get drunk more" - Drew '99

CLUB/ORGANIZATION DOES MOST FOR RU AND THE COMMUNITY

N.J. Public Interest Research Group Student Chapters (NJPIRG)

Contact: NJPIRG Student Chapters Office (732) 247-4606

"We are out there every day so one can't help but notice the difference we are making for the community. To date we have removed 15 tons of trash out of rivers across NJ, registered 10,000+ students to vote, have educated over 1,000 elementary school students on water quality issues, and worked with other Rutgers chapters to get 5 National Congressmen to sign an act to protect Endangered Species and their habitats. We're doing stuff, we're not just talking about it." - Allison Gertel, junior

"It's nice to feel that the students appreciate us. We are always doing things and sometimes it's hard to get volunteers, so you don't know if anyone cares. But with this recognition, you know that people do." - Christine Edly, junior

"Water Watch is designed to educate students and the community and to get them involved in helping out the NJ waterways." - Greg Visicaro, senior

2. Rutgers College Program Council (RCPC)
932-7213

3. Rutgers College Governing Association
932-6978

4. The Daily Targum
932-7051

5. Residence Hall Presidents Council
932-7209

6. The Community Service House
932-8660

7. The Greek Community
932-7692

8. The Medium
932-8197

9. (Tie) Children's AIDS Network (CAN) / Scarlet Key
932-9327 / 932-7731

10. RU with the Homeless / Habitat for Humanity
445-2894

"Piss in the sink Watchdog group" - '98   "Coca-Cola" - Steve
"Targum (they inform us and let us know about the other
groups and events on campus - without them we wouldn't know
about a lot of the worthwhile things there are around us)." - '99
"Facilities Maintenance" - Eric   "They all do" - Claire '99

BEST FRATERNITY TO JOIN
Chi Psi

"I feel very honored by the students response to us being the best fraternity to join. We work very hard to try and make Chi Psi an educational place with our leadership and social action programs, as well as making it a place to kick back and have fun.

"Our traditions foster the characteristics of manhood, and because of this I feel that we are the most respectful fraternity here at Rutgers. We treat everybody that steps through our doors as a guest and we don't go around badmouthing other fraternities. What is also great about us is how diverse we are both ethnically and in terms of our ambitions."

- Courtney Mather, chapter president

2. (Tie) Sigma Phi Epsilon / Zeta Psi

3. Chi Phi

4. Alpha Sigma Phi

5. Pi Kappa Alpha

6. Delta Phi

7. Omega Psi Phi

8. Phi Kappa Sigma

9. Kappa Sigma

10. Phi Kappa Tau

"Phi Smoka Fatty" - '98   "I hate Greek life" - '99
"None, not interested in AA" - '00   "Tap Akeg Aday" - '99
"Pie Omega Tau - POT" - '98   "Cumma Tappa Kegga"
"Lamda Lamda Lamda"   "Any that gives free beer" - '01

BEST SORORITY TO JOIN

Zeta Tau Alpha

"I am so happy that the students recognized us as the best sorority to join because we all work so hard to come across in a positive way. It is nice that the students can look beyond the stereotypes and give us this honor.

"There are all different types of girls that join ZTA. We have girls that are athletes and girls that are in the honors society. We are beyond looking at physical appearances, and focus on well rounded individuals that have a variety of extra carricular activities.

"The Greek system is a great thing to get involved in regardless of which sorority one joins. You get out of it whatever you put into it and the effort does pay off in the future." - Karen Novak, chapter president

2. Delta Gamma

3. Sigma Delta Tau

4. Sigma Kappa

5. Phi Sigma Sigma

6. Gamma Phi Beta

7. Delta Sigma Theta

8. Alpha Chi Omega

9. Mu Kappa Alpha

10. Lamda Theta Alpha

"the ones without the snotty blondes...wait, nevermind" - '01
"PMS" - Behrang '97   "Delta Delta Delta"   "STD" - '00
"None! Degrading form of socialization" - Melissa '98
"Zip Zero Zilch"   "none, why pay to have friends?" - '00

BEST FRATERNITY PARTY
Chi Psi

"Our rooms are always packed with people. We have a great girl to guy ratio - we don't believe in sausage parties. Also, we are always gentlemen to all of our guests. There is a variety of people that come here, lots of great music and a real nice house. Plus, we have a great sense of humor."
- Chi Psi brothers

2. Zeta Psi

3. Sigma Phi Epsilon

4. Kappa Sigma

5. Delta Phi

6. Alpha Sigma Phi

7. Chi Phi

8. (Tie) Theta Chi / Phi Kappa Sigma

9. Phi Delta Theta

10. Gamma Sig

"What's a frat party? All frats are on probation" - Chris '00   "Kai High" - '99
"can't remember, hungover" - '00   "The one where I had 20 beers"
"The ones where the guys don't grope you...wait, nevermind" - '01
"Around the world" - '01   "Do they still have parties?" - '01   "canceled one"
"Any frat with a big dance floor and good cheap beer" - '00   "Blue Whale"

WORST FRATERNITY PARTY
Sigma Alpha Mu

Random insight:

The nice thing about a dull party is that you get to bed at a decent hour.

2. Alpha Chi Ro

3. Chi Psi

4. Sigma Phi Epsilon

5. Zeta Psi

6. Theta Chi

7. (Tie) Alpha Sigma Phi / Phi Delta Theta

8. Tau Kappa Epsilon

9. Alpha Kappa Lamda

10. Alpha Epsilon Pi

"All - Middle School dances all over again" - '01   "Take your pick" - Rob '98
"the one where I had 20 beers"   "one that runs out of beer!!" - Stacey '99
"1,000 way tie, every one I've ever been to" - Ed '97   "Cramped basement"
"The ones where 100 guys stand around in little circles" - Amy '00
"Rhetorical Question" - Mike '99   "no such thing exists" - '98

FAVORITE BAR
Olde Queens Tavern
108 Easton Avenue - New Brunswick
(732) 846-4006

"It is very flattering to be chosen as the best bar by the students. We hope to continue to do the best job possible to meet the needs of our clients. We try to provide a comfortable environment for everyone, and our clientele make the best of it by interacting with each other as well as with the staff.

"In regards to being chosen as one of the top one hundred college bars in the nation by *Playboy Magazine*, it is another flattering honor. It is just another reflection upon how the clientele and the staff make this such a great place."   - Frank Sciotto, owner

2. The Knight Club
164 Easton Ave. New Brunswick 246-1551

3. Scarlet Pub
131 Easton Ave. New Brunswick 247-4771

4. The Melody
106 French St. New Brunswick 249-3784

5. The Golden Rail Pub
66 Easton Ave. New Brunswick 846-6279

6. Marita's Cantina
Ferren Deck Mall New Brunswick 247-3840

7. Ale 'N Wich
246 Hamilton St. New Brunswick 246-9178

8. Harvest Moon
392 George St. New Brunswick 249-6666

9. McCormick's Pub
266 Somerset St. New Brunswick 247-7822

10. Plum Street Pub
210 Hamilton St. New Brunswick 247-7822

"I like candy bars (Nestle Crunch, etc.)" - '98
"The Knight Club to dance, McCormick's to hang out, and the Melody for the exotic" - Heather '98
"None - I don't have ID yet" - '01   "Bar-Mitzvah" - '96

BEST BAR SPECIAL

Beat the Clock
@ The Knight Club

164 Easton Avenue - New Brunswick
(732) 246-1551

$1.00 Pitchers @ 8 PM
$2.00 Pitchers 10 - 12
$3.00 Pitchers 12 - Closing

$2.00 Jumbo Ice Teas and Well Drinks

2. $1.00 pitchers

3. Tuesday Night $1.00 pitchers
@ Plum Street Pub

4. (Tie) 50¢ drafts / $2.00 pitchers

5. (Tie) $1.00 mixed drinks / $1.00 drafts

6. 1¢ drafts @ Scarlet Pub

7. $1.00 kamikazes @ Marita's Cantina

8. Thursday Night free wings
@ Olde Queens Tavern

9. Tuesday Night 50¢ drafts
@ Marita's Cantina

10. Thursday Ladies Night - free mug
@ Olde Queens Tavern

"Never know, some guy always buys me the drinks" - Kim '00
"Screwdrivers for 50¢ for breakfast" - Mary Beth '99   "Free Cable TV"
"Penny till ya pee - all drafts are 1¢ until the first guy goes to the
bathroom" - Oliver '99   "Park Cafe shot of the week" - '98
"Get to know the bartender - cheap/free drinks" - Jessica '98
"Watching South Park Wed. night at the Ale 'N Wich" - Heather
"All beer is special"   "Wendy's super bar $4.99 all you can eat"
"doing 21 shots on your 21st b-day and they clean up the puke"

BEST BEER

Corona

"I like it with lime. It has a
light taste, not too heavy, reminds
me of Cancun and gets me drunk."
-Jamie Lawless, senior

2. Heineken

3. J.W. Dundee's Honey Brown

4. Coors Light

5. Sam Adams (assorted)

6. Natural Light

7. Guiness

8. Budweiser

9. Rolling Rock

10. Molson Ice

"Umm... I don't know - I haven't tried them all...yet" - Jesse '00
"Free" - Liliana '98   "Anything in a pitcher for $1.00"   "any available"
"I don't drink beer (don't forget us)" - '00   "Beer is for wussies" - '99
"Pot is less dangerous than beer" - '99   "Climax ESB at McCormick's"
"straight from a funnel"   "This is a dry dorm so naturally...Bud Dry" - '01
"Corona on payday, Milwaukee's Best every other day" - Kevin '98
"Natural Light - you'll learn to love it...it's cheap!" - '00   "Root beer"
"Scarlet Red at Harvest Moon" - '98   "beer is disgusting" - Katie '00
"Natural Ice - cheap staple for the hardcore drinker, with the highest
 percentage of alcohol" - '99   "Birch beer"   "Weis, er, weis, bud" - '99
"the one you have right before the last one you can handle" - '96

BEST PLACE TO HAVE SEX

Bed / Bedroom

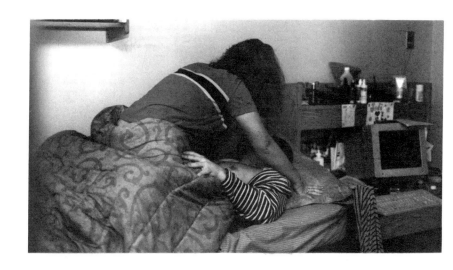

Quotations on sex

"Sex has become one of the most discussed subjects of modern times. The Victorians pretended it did not exist; the moderns pretend that nothing else exists". - Fulton J. Sheen

"Is sex dirty? Only if it's done right." - Woody Allen

"Whoever called it necking was a poor judge of anatomy."
 - Groucho Marx

2. In the dorm (lounge, balcony, stairwell...)

3. In the shower

4. In the bathroom

5. In the library

6. In the laundry room

7. On your roommate's bed

8. On the beach

9. In a classroom

10. In the car

"Scott Hall 135 - not that I ever have but its a damn good place" - '00
"every place is a great place to have sex" - '99   "Under Silent Willie" - '99
"976 numbers" - '00   "Why would I tell you, you might steal my ideas" - '00
"on the banks of the Old Raritan" - '00   "Not married...wouldn't know" - '00
"50-yard line of stadium" - '00   "behind random houses on Ray Street" - '98
"Busch Campus Tray Conveyor (after hours)" - '01   "The SAC front desk"
"Top floor lounge of the CORE building after hours" - '98   "Car wash" - '01
"Places where if you get caught, you'll get in big trouble (or really
  embarassed)" - 99   "Anywhere - as long as you use a condom every time!"
"Let you know when I get some..." - '99   "The wobbly bridge on DC" - '99
"Grandparents House" - '00   "anywhere people are watching" - '98
"quiet study lounge in Hardenburgh Hall 1, but you may get rug burns" - '98
"Belmar - on the beach under the boardwalk" - '98   "Radio City Music Hall"
"no public areas; in private & only with someone you love and cherish" - '98
"bench on the corner of Somerset and College Ave." - '98   "my pants"

BEST FESTIVAL AT RUTGERS

Ag Field Day

"We are very proud that the students of Rutgers have chosen this program as the best festival at Rutgers. On April 25th, 1998, we will have had the 80th Ag Field Day at Cook College, formerly the College of Agriculture and Environmental Science and the College of Agriculture.

"Ag Field Day is the showcase for Cook College, when the campus is opened up to the greater community of parents, alumni, and guests to enjoy its environmental beauty. It is very attractive to the students because it is put together by the members of the Cook community and provides entertainment, food, and the opportunity to see what the Cook academic departments and clubs have to offer." - Dean Lee Schneider, Dean of Students for Cook College

2. Rutgersfest

3. Homecoming

4. Unity Day

5. Coming Out Day

6. Springfest

7. Caribbean Rec Fest

8. Buschfest

9. Harmony Day

10. Octoberfest

"It used to be Ag Field Day until they (authority figures) basically ruined it. They are trying to make this University a dry campus. Everything used to be so much crazier: fun. Now it is not. I really feel bad for the incoming classes that are going through Rutgers. They have nothing to do." - '98 "Smokefest" - '99   "graduation" - Tom '01   "end of school" "Drinking until you puke in your room fest" - Mike '98

BEST LOCAL BAND
Fatty Lumpkin

169 Fresh Ponds Road
Jamesburg, NJ 08831
Band Members: Erik, Steve, Mike, Pete, and Scott

"We're pretty excited that the students recognized us as being the best local band. It's really great that they have heard our music and appreciate it. Hey, there is nothing better than when people get together to drink and smoke and listen to us. People have told us that we sound similar to the Allman Brothers but we know that we have our own distinct sound. It is a compilation of many bands out there, and combined it makes up our own great music." - Fatty Lumpkin band members

2. Evelyn Forever

The Airplay Label, PO Box 851, Asbury Park, NJ 07712

3. Velour

13 High St., New Brunswick 08901 / (732) 448-0171 Pete Novembre

4. Roger's Sparrow

*****

5. Victor Diggs and the Boogie Love

(732) 418-9090 - Brian or Damian / (516) 747-2455 Damian or Bill

6. The Good Life

1935 5th St., North Brunswick 08903 / thegoodlife@erols.com

7. Gabriel's Hold

******

8. Inspector 7

****

9. Bionic Rhoda

Powerbunny 4x4 Records, PO Box 792, New Brunswick 08903
scavone@rci.rutgers.edu

10. Exit-9

66 Suydam St. - Apt. 1, New Brunswick 08903
(732) 247-5624 Thomas or Xavier

What do you think this is, Seattle?" - '00

BEST JERSEY TOWN TO COME FROM

Cherry Hill

"We're glad that Rutgers University students recognize what we've always known - that Cherry Hill is a wonderful place to grow up. Like Rutgers, our town offers an excellent education, lots of activity, and an environment that encourages people to succeed."
- Mayor Susan Bass Levin

2. East Brunswick

3. Jersey City

4. Newark

5. Edison

6. Randolph

7. Old Bridge

8. Freehold

9. Marlboro

10. (Tie) Kearny / Princeton

"none - everyone in Jersey drives a Camaro - come from CT like me!" - Bonnie '99   "anywhere northeast - NY influence" - '98 "Out of state, baby!!!" - Wendi '98   "is there such a thing?" - '00 "anywhere in North Jersey" - '98   "Exit 16E on the Turnpike" "anything above the (609) area code"   "anywhere on the shore"

The Rutgers Students Unofficial Guide to College

Sports

BEST TEAM

Men's Soccer

Coach: Bob Reasso

1997 Season Record

14 - 7 - 2

Big East Champions

2. Men's Basketball

3. Field Hockey

4. Football

5. Women's Basketball

6. Baseball

7. Men's Crew

8. Volleyball

9. Dance Team

10. Women's Lacrosse

"Sexy silk boxer wearing Basketball team" - Sophie '99
"one that actually wins" - Tom '00   "Chess" - '01
"beer olympics" "College is about academics, not sports" - '99
"cutest team - Girls Soccer" - '99   "Football (despite season)"

WORST TEAM

Football

Coach: Terry Shae

1997 Season Record

0 Wins - 11 Losses

In all fairness to the football team, who played their hearts out on the field, but could not muster up a win, this is their season in review (explaining why it was the only team with more than one vote for worst team).

8/30/97 - Virginia Tech 59 Rutgers 19
9/6/97 - Rutgers 14 Texas 48
9/13/97 - Rutgers 7 Navy 36
9/20/97 - Boston College 35 Rutgers 21
10/4/97 - Rutgers 0 West Virginia 48
10/9/97 Syracuse 50 Rutgers 3
10/18/97 - Rutgers 35 Army 37
10/25/97 - Pittsburgh 55 Rutgers 48
11/1/97 - Rutgers 7 Temple 49
11/8/97 - Wake Forest 28 Rutgers 14
11/15/97 - Rutgers 23 Miami 51

However, in all fairness to those who filled out surveys,
here are their comments:

"As if you don't know - hut, hut... 0-12" - '99   "Unfortunately, football"
"Football (we spend too much money on a team that sucks)" - '98
"I think you know" - '98   "Football - no further explanation needed!"
"Must you ask (football)" - '99   "Football players (but they try)" - '98
"Football, football, football" - '98   "Do I have to say? (Football)" - '98
"You answer that. I'll give you a hint, they lost 11 games straight" - '01
"Hmmm...let's see...maybe FOOTBALL!" - '01   "Gee...I wonder" - '00
"Dumb Question" - '01   "Are you serious!?" - '98   "Take a guess"
"Football = they suck!"   "R U kidding??"   "Clearly football"
"Gee let me think...football" - '01   "Come on now, Football" - '01
"Men's Football...pathetic" - '99   "Umm? Football of course" - '00
"It's a given (0-11) Hint Hint" - '00   "Football (Duh!)" -'98

BEST COACH
Kevin Bannon

Men's Basketball

"Obviously, I'm the new kid on the block and right now I am really enjoying my honeymoon period. It's nice to see that the students appreciate what I bring to the table and what my vision is of what this place can become. I have always found that if you want people around you to be supportive and to follow your lead, it can only be gotten through a work ethic that is second to nobody. That's what I try to be all about.

"In terms of the team, if you look at places like U Mass and U Conn and the great resources they have as state universities, those teams exploded with the right leadership. The same is going to happen here at Rutgers." - Kevin Bannon

2. Bob Reasso
Men's Soccer

3. Vivan Stringer
Women's Basketball

4. Terry Shae
Football

5. Fred Hill
Baseball

6. Anne Marie Petracco
Field Hockey

7. Christine Zoffinger
Dance Team

8. Tom Hayes
Men's Lacrosse

9. John Sacchi
Wrestling

10. Roberta Anthes
Women's Track and Field

"The one that screams the most"   "they all need to be replaced" - '98
"Coach from Cheers" - '00   "Whoever is not the football coach" - Mary '99
"Me (Go team go!!)" - '99   "Can't replace Wenzel" - Jeannine '98
"Don't know any, therefore they make too much money" - '00   "Tuna!!" - '98
"Greyhound because it takes you where you want to go to" - '98

BEST SPORT
TO WATCH
Basketball

"Basketball is the best sport to watch because it is exciting, fast paced, and there is always action. It is very electrifying and the fans really get in to it. Each sport has their own characteristics, positives and negatives, but in my opinion basketball is the best to watch." - Mike Jasnosz, senior

2. Soccer

3. Football

4. Lacrosse

5. Ice Hockey

6. Baseball

7. Volleyball

8. Rugby

9. Swimming

10. Tennis

"The visiting Football team" - '01   "Shuffleboard" - John '00
"full-contact tiddlywinks" - '01   "Synchronized blinking" - '01
"Bong team" - '99   "No Hold Barred Fighting" - '98
"don't ever go to Rutgers games" - '98   "Darts" - '99
"Sports with men in tight pants" - '00   "Mud Wrestling" - '99
"Frat guys trying to get some" - Tony '97   "funneling" - '98
"chess championship on ESPN" "football - loaded of course"

BEST RECREATIONAL SPORT TO PLAY

Volleyball

"Whether it is beach or indoor volleyball, two person or six person, recreational or competitive, the numerous versions of volleyball attract a wide variety of players who help make it one of the fastest growing sports today. Volleyball's simplicity makes it an easy sport for novice players to learn and play, which makes it a very enjoyable rec sport. For the more advanced player, however, volleyball helps to physically condition and continuously challenge even the most veteran player to master the game. In other words, its an awesome sport for just about anyone.

"The Sonny Werblin Rec Center, on Busch Campus is the most popular place to find an indoor or outdoor volleyball game. Pick-up games can be found on almost any weeknight, but for stronger competition, Tuesday and Thursday tend to attract more experienced players." - Allen Hua, Founder of Rutgers ASVBA

2. Soccer

3. Basketball

4. Ultimate Frisbee

5. Football

6. Tennis

7. Roller & Floor Hockey

8. Softball

9. Flag Football

10. Racquetball

"Tightrope walking balancing a piano & an elephant while singing the national anthem backwards" - Tom   "boy watching"   "Man Hunt" - '98
"Frisbee Golf" - Laurie '00   "Does running for buses count?" - '01
"Teatherball" - Willie   "Co-Ed Naked Twister" - '99   "Pinball"
"Recreational use of drugs" - '00   "Hackey Sack" - '01   "Pitfall" - '98
"pocket pool" - '99   "Beer pong" - Heather '00   "Badminton" - '00
"whiffleball" - '96   "Naked wrestling (oh, that's sex!)" - Susan '98
"Freestyle masturbation" - '98   "Recreational chemistry" - Brian '00

YOUR MIND CAN'T CONTROL YOUR BODY, RIGHT?

EVER BEEN SCARED?

Think about it. You're in an unnerving situation. Your heart races and you can feel the blood rushing through your arteries. Then you begin to feel those familiar "butterflies in the stomach" just as the adrenaline starts to pour into your muscles, making them tense with excess energy.

In stressful situations our minds attempt to control our bodies in ways similar to this one. And after repeated episodes, it can begin to take its toll on all the body's systems, often contributing to heart problems, digestive tract disorders, chronic pain, insomnia, infertility and a breakdown of the immune system.

At the Mind/Body Medical Institute at St. Peter's Medical Center, we're using methods developed at the Mind/Body Medical Institute of Beth Israel Deaconess Medical Center/Harvard Medical School to counteract stress-related medical conditions. Along with exercise and nutrition regimens, our clinical programs teach you how to relax and use your mind to affect your body in more positive ways. In conjunction with your doctor's care, these clinical programs can help speed your recovery by reducing the stress associated with your medical condition. We also offer programs for Chronic Pain, Cancer, Infertility, Cardiac Risk Reduction, Healthy Lifestyles for people with Diabetes, Insomnia, Menopause and Healthy Lifestyles.

For more information, give us a call at (732) 937-6051.

The Mind/Body Medical Institute at St. Peter's
an affiliate of the Mind/Body Medical Institute of Beth Israel Deaconess Medical Center/Harvard Medical School.

St. Peter's
Medical Center & Health System
Nobody knows more about healing.

A Catholic Hospital Sponsored by the Diocese of Metuchen

THE HOSPITAL FOR WOMEN & CHILDREN • THE CHILDREN'S HEALTH NETWORK
THE CANCER INSTITUTE OF NJ • UMDNJ-RWJ MEDICAL SCHOOL • ELDERCARE SERVICES
PARTNERS IN CARE • COMMUNITY CARE SERVICES

New Brunswick Life

BEST STORE TO SHOP AT
Etc Company
120 Albany Street - New Brunswick
(732) 846-1002

"The greatest thing about Etc is it's always changing. The owners adapt to the diversity of both the students and the staff. The products resemble this because they come from all over the world. Even the music in the store is multi-cultural and hip. Many of the products represent having an open mind and a feeling of goodness. There are light-hearted things as well as more serious gifts to fit the needs of every customer. We also believe that shopping should be fun, and therefore encourage people to touch the items." - Francis Paulino, manager

"Great knickknacks and cool stuff!" - Colleen, senior

2. Finale
120 Albany St. New Brunwick 828-2122

3. Cheap Thrills
121 Somerset St. New Brunswick 246-2422

4. Rutgers University Bookstore
Ferren Deck Mall New Brunswick 246-8448

5. Vintage Image Boutique
29-B Easton Ave. New Brunswick 246-7667

6. (Tie) Up in Smoke / Sam Goody
53 Mine St. 846-6370 / 4 Easton Ave. 435-0187

7. Bloom's
98 Albany St. New Brunswick 246-0818

8. SAC Convenience Store
613 George St. New Brunswick 214-9069

9. Rite-Aid Pharmacy
360 George St. New Brunswick 247-0814

10. Planet X
43 Easton Ave. New Brunswick 249-0304

"Cliquers - Inexpensive clothes, OK wigs - It's a funny
experience, a guaranteed laugh" - Jeannine '98
"No money to shop" - David '99   "Adult Novelty Shop" - '99
"roommate's closet" - '00   "inexpensive" - '00
"Hurtado Health Center for cheap condoms" - Eugene

MOST RUTGERS FRIENDLY STORE

Rutgers University Bookstore

1 Penn Plaza - Ferren Deck Mall New Brunswick
(732) 246-8448

"We are thrilled to be chosen as the most Rutgers friendly store because the Rutgers students and the faculty are our main focus. Our goal is to be the retailer of choice for the Rutgers students. Certainly we want to be their first choice and the best choice and we are thrilled to be recognized."
- Barry Brown, store director

2. Scarlet Fever
109 Somerset St. New Brunswick 247-4678

3. SAC Convenience Store
613 George St. New Brunswick 214-9069

4. New Jersey Books
108 Somerset St. New Brunswick 828-7401

5. Etc Company
120 Albany St. New Brunswick 846-1002

6. Thomas Sweet
55 Easton Ave. New Brunswick 828-3855

7. Scarlet Knotes
119 Somerset St. New Brunswick 247-3399

8. Student Co-op Bookstore
57 Lipman Dr. New Brunswick 932-9017

9. (Tie) Campus Deli / Jimmy's Grille Specialite
82 Senior St. 828-4011 / 104 Easton Ave. 418-9600

10. (Tie) Up in Smoke / Joe's Liquors
53 Mine St. 846-6370 / 160 Louis St. 846-2244

"Hole in the Wall - owners are super-friendly" - '98
"any place that accepts Knight Express" - '01   "any on Easton"
"Joe (Joe's Liquors) is the friendliest guy I have ever met!" - Rich
"any place with a discount for students" - '98   "student loans"
"with out a doubt...Princeton University Bookstore" - Glenn '01

BEST PLACE
TO WORSHIP
St. Peter's R C Church

(Catholic Center at Rutgers uses St. Peter's Church for masses)

94 Somerset Street - New Brunswick (732) 545-6820

"We are absolutely thrilled to be chosen. The Catholic Center is a warm place where we provide support for students in all aspects of their lives. We are a welcoming community for Catholics and non-Catholics alike.

"The majority of students come to the Campus Ministry mass at St. Peter's Church on Sunday evenings at 10pm." - Father Joseph Celano, Catholic Center Chaplain

2. Chabad House
170 College Ave. New Brunswick 296-1800

3. Kirkpatrick Cathedral
85 Somerset St. New Brunswick 932-7808

4. Hillel Foundation
93 College Ave. New Brunswick 545-2407

5. St. Michael's Chapel
40 Davidson Road Piscataway 932-3218

6. Voorhees Chapel
Chapel Drive New Brunswick 932-9374

7. Rutgers Community Chinese Church
445 Ceder Grove Lane Somerset 469-0611

8. Muslim Center of Middlesex County
1012 Hoes Lane Piscataway 463-2004

9. St. George Greek Orthodox Church
1101 River Road Piscataway 699-9894

10. Anshe Emeth Memorial Temple
222 Livingston Ave. New Brunswick 545-6484

"in your heart" - Araxi '97   "at the temple of the porcelain god"
"In front of the classroom right before your final" - Kevin '98   "the sidewalk"
"In my basement with candles" - '98   "the alter to Elvis in my room"
"From any bed - Sunday morning, hung over"   "anywhere you're comfy"
"w/ one of the many cults here at RU" - '98   "at the feet of Fran Lawrence"
"secret tunnels connecting Frats to the Raritan" - Alex '98   "feet of a model"

BEST PLACE TO VOLUNTEER
Robert Wood Johnson
University Hospital
One Robert Wood Johnson Place - New Brunswick
(732) 937-8507
Contact: Donna Miceli

"It is an honor to say that we are the best place to volunteer at Rutgers. I am not surprised though because we are the premier academic medical institution.

"As director, I make sure I know the needs and the wants of the volunteers and try to get them to match. We have positions in the emergency room, the child life program doing arts and crafts with kids, the patient information desk greeting visitors and escorting patients, and in other various departments doing a variety of chores.

"Volunteerism is coming back in style and there's a great importance in lending a hand." - Donna Miceli, Director of Volunteer Services

2. St. Peter's Medical Center
254 Easton Ave. New Brunswick 745-8600 / Contact: Michelle Gaskel Ext. 8573

3. Elijah's Promise Soup Kitchen
18 Neilson New Brunswick 545-9002 / Contact: Marvin Taylor 545-9373

4. Big Buddy @ New Brunswick School
Contact: Rutgers Community Outreach 932-7823

5. Catholic Center
17 Mine St. New Brunswick 545-6663 / Contact: Sister Jeanne Goyette

6. Citizenship and Service Education (CASE)
78 College Ave. New Brunswick 932-8660 / Contact: Michael Shafer

7. Children's AIDS Network
CAC, Student Activities Center Box #69 932-9327 / Contact: Stephen Bromer

8. RU w/ the Homeless / Habitat for Humanity
Contact: Peter Sobel 445-2894

9. NJ Public Interest Research Group Student Chapters
Contact: NJPIRG Student Chapters Office 247-4606

10. Douglass Developmental Disabilities Center
25 Gibbons Circle New Brunswick 932-9137 / Contact: Maria Arnold

---

"in class, open your house up to a study group, can turn into a night of fun" - '99   "our generation is too apathetic to volunteer" - '01 "a sleep study" - '00   "Place where you get paid for it" - Tom "Helping football team" - '01   "internships in your major" - Carol-Ann "RWJ - especially when they pay you 20 bucks an hour to be a model to practice physicals on!!" - Mary '00   "Up in Smoke" - '00

The Rutgers Students Unofficial Guide to College

Life on campus

MOST HELPFUL OFFICE/DEPT.

Rutgers College General Honors Program

Milledoler Hall - Room 210, CAC
(732) 932-7964

"We are honored to have been chosen as the most helpful office. It is important to us that all students, not just those in the General Honors Program, feel that this office is a place where they can get help, and being chosen as the most helpful office suggests that this message has been communicated. "
- Muffin Lord, director

2. Office of the Dean
Milledoler Hall, CAC 932-7025

3. Rutgers Campus Information Services
932-INFO

4. English Department
104 Murray Hall, CAC 932-7633

5. Office of Academic Services
Milledoler Hall, CAC 932-7731

6. Communication Department
207 & 208 4 Huntington St. (SCILS), CAC 932-8563

7. Financial Aid Office
Records Hall - Room 140, CAC 932-7057

8. Journalism Department
108 4 Huntington St., CAC 932-8567

9. Hurtado Health Center
11 Bishop Place, CAC 932-7401

10. Office of Career Services
46 College Ave., CAC 932-7997

"When I find one, I'll let you know" - Mary '00
"Hurtado - cheap condoms"   "No such thing"

LEAST HELPFUL OFFICE/DEPT.

Parking and Transportation Services

26 Mine Street, CAC
(732) 932-8117

"I stopped buying parking passes because it is easier to get tickets and mail them in than it is to wait on line to get a parking permit. When you do show up, they are quite indifferent and in fact, you're last on their list in terms of priorities."
-Jason Swain, senior

2. Financial Aid Office
Records Hall - Room 140, CAC 932-7057

3. Office of the Registrar
Administrative Services Building, BC 445-2757

4. Office of Academic Services
104 Murray Hall, CAC 932-7731

5. Office of the Dean
Milledoler Hall, CAC 932-7025

6. Rutgers College Housing Office
Clothier Hall, CAC 932-7017

7. Mathematics Department
303 Hill Center, BC 445-2390

8. Hurtado Health Center
11 Bishop Place, CAC 932-7401

9. Chemistry Department
150 Wright/Reimann Laboratory, BC 445-2604

10. Office of Fraternity and Sorority Affairs
15 Bartlett St., CAC 932-7692

"Can you say RU Screw?" - Amy '98   "too close to call" - Sarah '01
"I don't think the phones work properly between depts. because not one of
 them has a clue as to what's going on with the others" - Sal '99 "the meter maids"
"All...so impolite" - '01   "None. They are all mediocer like my spelling!" - '00
"(the) 'we don't really do anything, no matter what you tell us' dept." - '01
"Financial Aid - do you really think someone wants to help you get more $" - Denny
"Rutgers College Deans office - every office shuffles you around to the next that
 you are basically a bothersome piece of shit" - '98   "Take your pick" - Jake '99

BEST TARGUM SECTION/COLUMN

Horoscopes

"I rely on the *Targum* horoscopes so much that if my day is below a 6, I go right back to bed."
- Tracey Mattia, senior

"My horoscope tells me that I'll find true love every other day...I'm still single."
- Bob Thagliente, senior

2. Crossword Puzzle

3. Police Blotter

4. Comics

5. Sports

6. Word Jumble

7. Inside Beat

8. Classified

9. Opinion/Editorial

10. Front Page

"The crossword puzzle, great way to pass classtime!" - '99
"any that makes me laugh and are written with honesty" - '99
"Beer specials" - Christine, '98   "the corrections"
"I don't read that smut"   "The one anti-liberal column a year"

BEST WRSU SHOW (88.7 FM)
Sports Events

"This is a real compliment because it comes directly from the students. We always strive to be the best at the station, and in general. The mere fact that we were voted number one shows that we're deep in our ability and that we're likable. Everyone on the staff should take a share in the credit." - Rich DeMarco, sports

"I think WRSU Sports provides an opportunity for people who dream of persuing a career in radio and even for those who don't, but just love sports. It is a great way to be a part of the athletic program here at Rutgers. I've gotten the chance to travel around the country and interview a lot of great coaches and players and host a talk show." - Erica Herskowitz, sportscaster

2. Jazz from the Hub

3. Soccer Magazine

4. Radio Ruckus

5. Newscasts

6. Knight Line

7. The Blueprint w/ Ashan

8. Knightbeat

9. Infinite Ends

10. Land of the Shakers

"Don't even know where to find this on my radio"
"WRS...what?"   "The day D.J. Delight sheds his light" - '99
"Cultural shows" - Amritha, '00   "What's a WRSU?"
"Huh! Doesn't come in, in my room" - '01   "Dead Air Shows"

BEST BUS

EE (accordian)

From College Avenue
to Douglass/Cook via Neilson Street

"It is so big that there are really good odds of getting a seat to sit down in. You are not packed in like cattle like you are in the other buses. Also, you don't have to wait that long for the EE buses. And the drivers are pretty friendly also."
   -Liz, Emma, and Jen, freshman

2. A

3. H

4. LX

5. F

6. EE

7. L

8. GG

9. B

10. Security Shuttle

"EE large catepiller like double buses" - Dave '98   "empty ones" - '01
"Hahahahahaha!!" - '98   "Any that actually use the excellorator" - '99
"Crazy Jamaican bus drivers' route" - '98   "Hawaiin Tropics' bus"
"Thank God I'm a senior and have a car" - '98   "EE extenda bus"
"Canni bus" - Dana '98   "The ones that are on schedule" - Melissa
"Uh...depends on driver" - '00   "EE - who doesn't love the swivel" - '01
"The air conditioned L" - Jamie '98   "M14 - I can go to the mall!"
"EE because it's the only bus you can greet the driver in when the bus
 makes a turn" - '01   "A - with the bus driver that whistles" - Darcy '99
"Doesn't apply. These words can't go together in same sentence"
"ones that don't break down!!" - '97   "Security Shuttle -Drunk Cart"
"EE with the tilt-a-whirl in the middle"   "the ones that go to New York"

BEST PLACE TO SIT OUTSIDE

Voorhees Mall

College Avenue Campus

"Voorhees Mall is the best place to sit outside because there's lots of open grassy space where you can lie down, read a book or run around and play frisbee. It is one of the few open spaces in an otherwise urban town. It feels good to replenish the soul by relaxing there on a day filled with classes."
- Carrie Budoff, senior

2. Passion Puddle

3. House porch

4. Bishop Beach

5. Buccleuch Park

6. Au Bon Pain

7. Rutgers Student Center

8. Busch Suites Courtyard (Magic Circle)

9. Deiner Park

10. Brower Courtyard

"on that silly wooden porch in front of Alexander Library" - '98
"under a tree, next to squirrels" - Angie '99   "my roof" - Ian '98
"bus stop" - '00 "my front porch if our chair wasn't stolen" - '99
"who wants to sit in goose shit" - Dan '01   "Rt. 18 - in the middle"
"Front steps of a frat, loaded out of your mind"   "anywhere" - '99

BEST LOOKING BUILDING

Old Queens

Did you know...

Old Queens was built in 1809 and was originally called the Queens Building, named after King George III's wife, Charlotte Sophia.

2. Murray Hall
College Avenue Campus

3. Bishop House
College Avenue Campus

4. Kirkpatrick Cathedral
College Avenue Campus

5. Johnson & Johnson Building
College Avenue Campus

6. Art History Library
College Avenue Campus

7. Sonny Werblin Recreation Center
Busch Campus

8. Serin Physics Lab
Busch Campus

9. University Center at Easton Avenue
College Avenue Campus

10. Hill Center
Busch Campus

"Most on Douglass - historic ones"
"the one on the credit card" "non-classrooms"

BEST STATUE/ MONUMENT
Willie the Silent

Legend of Willie the Silent:

The statue of William, Prince of Orange, has stood at the end of Voorhees Mall since 1928. The piece is a replica of a statue erected in Holland's Hague museum by artist Lodewyk Royer in 1848. In 1926, the Holland Society of New York gave the statue of Willie to Rutgers intending it to serve as a symbol of the College's Dutch roots. Tradition has it that Willie whistles whenever a virgin walks by his post. Tradition also has it that he has not whistled once since he's been here at Rutgers.

2. Nixon
In front of Brower Commons

3. Dark Elergy
Douglass Campus

4. Split and Twisted
In front of SERC I

5. James Suydam
Seminary Place

6. Reflections
Near the Engineering Building

7. Football Comemoration
In front of football stadium

8. Mason Gross Memorial
In front of Milledoler Hall

9. Vietnam Memorial
Near Scott Hall, CAC

10. Alexander Library Landscape
In front of Alexander Library

"Thing outside Livingston Student Center"   "Rocky Monument" - '00
"that dude" - '98   "The 13 inch Bronze Penis on Douglass" - '98
"The one they will make of me someday" - '01   "erected by his friends"
"The one that is supposed to whistle at virgins, but he's never whistled at me"
"Willy the Saint"   "that ugly thing in front of Brower" - '00   "Henry the Silent"
"The statue of the orgy on Douglass" - Heath   "the fucked up thing at Brower"
"the smoke stack outside my window" - Tommy '00   "Whistling Willy"

WRSU FM NEW BRUNSWICK,

88.7 FM
WRSU
RUTGERS
University

A RADIO STATION.

ACKNOWLEGEMENTS

I have always tried to live by the words of John Casper Lavater. He stated that "He is incapable of a truly good action who finds not a pleasure in contemplating the good actions of others." Well not a day has gone by since I starting working on this book that I haven't looked forward to writing the acknowledgement section of this book, in order to thank everyone that helped me out in one way or another. From the bottom of my heart, I want to let you all know how much I appreciate all that you have done.

A special thanks to my brother *Phil* for all of his time and support in getting this project up and running. And to *Brenda* for being my favorite sister (and my only sister). Mom, Dad, thanks also.

Thanks to *Dave Leta* for a terrific job with the cover and with the company logo. I am lucky to have found such a talented individual.

To *Chris Yoon* of Fine 1 Hr. Photo in East Brunswick who worked with me very patiently in trying to teach me how to use my camera for black and white photographs and did the best job possible with the negatives that I gave to him.

Thanks to the following individuals that took that extra step to help distribute surveys, gather information, or just lent a helping hand when I needed one:
Marty Angstreich, Alex Barenbaum, Brian Bibenedetto, Carrie Budoff, Rob Chess, Kristy Gillio, Dan Hakim, Jill Hetman, Mitra Kalita, David Katz, Kristina Kersey, Dan Levine, Vic Perez, Jeanne Schumacker, Jodi Varon, and David Weintraub

Thanks to Chuck Berninger, Jason Redd, and the rest of the RHPC executive board for distributing surveys in the dorms. And also, thanks to the following hall presidents for returning them:
Mathew Rourke, Sagar Mehta, Deana Green, Jan Marc Quisumbly, Madeline Mayer, Marc Cohen, Deanielle Effenberger, Elizabeth Olacio, Maria Perez, Paula Vaszuez, Enid Soto, Amy Sisco, Amanda Brett, Nabil Shurafa, Rajiv Parikh, Kevin George, Charles Wond, Jose Laranjeiro, Katherine Juh, Stephanie Ross, Jennifer Ferry, and James Cartwright

Thanks to *Jessica Wohl, Josh Carr, and Becky Coyte* over at WRSU and *Tom Keaton* at *The Daily Targum*

Thank you to *Rabbi Baruch Goodman* at the Chabad House for allowing me to distribute surveys there and for being a friend to all.

Thanks to the following professors and Rutgers staff who offered me either their class time, their resources, their wisdom, and or their kindness:
Security Officer Archibold, Marsha Bergman, John Biser, Alma Blount, Susan Boyd, John Chapin, Maurice Charney, Paris DeSoto, Irving Horowitz, Kevin Kelly, Pete Kowalski Linda Lederman, Joe Mancuso, Steve Miller, Scott Novak, Dan Ogilvie, Jesse Rambo, Carol Savage, Elizabeth Winchester, and the Alexander Library Archives staff.

I also must give credit to *Larry Levanfi* for taking the picture of the men's soccer team on page 114, *Tony Cho* of *The Daily Targum* for taking the picture of Kevin Bannon on page 118, and to *Thomas Berenbrok* who took the Cherry Hill picture on page 110.
A special thanks to the folks at Campus Information (932-INFO) for answering my many questions

To all of you who filled out surveys and put your name, thank you:

Marisa Allen, Shana Alston, Amanda An, Katie Anderson, Jessica Antal, Anne-Marie Armata, Cristina Arnese, Ben Balikov, Alex Baker, Shoshana Bannett, Alison Barry, Fausto Batista, Robert Beck, Heather Behrens, Anna Belkin, Chris Bergamo, Jacob Betteridge, Nisha Bhatt, Leticia Bido, Monica Biskup, John Blase, Lucia Boatman, Michael Bober, Jennifer Bowlby, Keith Brenner, Channel Bryant, Eric Bryce, Gil Broyer, Michael Bruno, Christine Burk, Cecil Burr, Lara Calabrase, Nick Calafati, Mark Calder, Sandee Campbell, Tom Campolo, Glenn Canares, Jesse Cannella, Heather Carberry, Desiree Caro, Brian Carroll, Mayra Casal, Laurie Castiglia, Angie Catalano, Tracy Cedrone, Salvadore Chappman, Jordan Charney, Iwalani Ching, Tommy Chong, Raab Chosid, Lauren Chuebon, Robert Cicero, Dan Cifarelli, Mike Cobucci, Jeffrey Cohen, Jennifer Cohen, Christine Collins, Kim Conlon, Kim Consolino, Thomas Cook, Denise Cosenzo, Jeff Coyle, Averi Crane, Melissa Craddock, Renee Crivello, Limin Cruz, Michael Cuffe, Toni Czeczuga, Ed Daswani, Genia Daukshta, Kafi Davis, Mike Davis, Tara Day, Isabela Debek, Bob DeFortuna, Amanlis DeJesus, Jeannine DeMicco, Suchi Desai, Barron DeSantis, Jana Diamond, Miria Diaz, Kristen DiCerto, Ani DiFranco, Carmen DiMaio, Ed Ditmire, Mike DiPaulo, Rachel Dixon, Jen Dore, Amy Draemel, Jon Dubinsky, Christina Duca, Jennifer Dunn, Rachel Dunst, Catherine Durkin, Debbie Duyckinck, Tom Edge, Kevin Edwards, Heath Eliwatt, Zaki Enayethulilah, Veronica Escalona, Walend Esmail, Kristen Esposito, Brad Evans, Tammer Fakhrg, Rose Fanus, Heather Faunce, David Faustino, Brooke Feldman, Ike Fergusson, Michelle Ferrer, Steven Fidler, Bonnie Fineman, Sarah Finkelstein, Ron Fitch, Erica Flatley, Stephanie Fonseca, Lauren Franco, Jon Freitag, Greg Froehlich, Jennifer Gallagher, Stacey Gallino, Araxi Garabed, Susan Geevarghese, Lisa Gerber, Joan-Marie Giambo, Danielle Gilbert, Derek Gillespie, Leonardo Giorgi, Monica Glanvilee, Robyn Glassman, Chris Gliemlmi, Miriam Goldfine, Jim Goffred, Lauren Grabelle, Daniella Granata, Yomi Greenstein, Steven Gregov, Matt Gristina, Dave Grohl, Jennifer Grzywacz, Ross Guberman, Anthony Guida, Jennifer Hall, Darcy Hamilton, Rob Hannon, Vivian Harmon, Amber Hart, Jaime Hartwick, Heather Kaynes, Sophie Hazel, Lanna Hecht, Wendy Heller, Melissa Henderson, Erica Herskowitz, Tanisha Hicks, Ty Higgs, Janel Hileman, Nicole Hillenmayer, Rana Hilton, Eric Hines, Jenni Hoagland, Bob Hoban, Matthew Holder, Melissa Horowitz, Chris Hou, Lauren Iovino, Edna Ishayik, Lauren Jannicelli, Pintu Jinger, Deiara Johnson, Melissa Jones, Paul Joseph, Annetta Jurczenko, Eugene Jun, Lori Kahn, Abdullah Damadan, David Kanarek, Rebecca Karcher, Allyson Kasetta, Brenden Kavana, Mike Kavka, Nichole Keller, Colleen Kelly, Michele Kelly, Sanaz Khorsand, Jong Soo Kim, Ireng Kiouretzis, Lindsay Klein, Theodore Klein, Lisa Klimkiewicz, Susan Kline, Jack Kloster, Cyntia Kociban, Amritha Krishnan, Dara Kromenacker, Jeff Kuczynski, Asia Labrie, Esteve Laetitia, Melba Laguatan, Joshua Lane, Rachel Lang, Mary Laszczuk, Katie Latshaw, Andy Lau, Emily Lawler, Kairida Layton, Fred LeBlanc, Jen Lee, Janis Lemke, Nathalie Lenais, John Leone, Cari Levy, Nicole Lieb, Faith Lieberman, Gil Lieblich, Nancy Lindsley, Allsion Linfante, Melissa Lipkin, Lainie Lippin, Erik Lister, Elana Loewenthal, Nevada Longshore, Carolee Lowry, Jamie Luchs, Francis Luk, Mike Lusto, Jeff Mack, James Mackey, Jeff Magnuson, Dan Maldonado, Amy Manegold, Luna Mann, Jennifer Mantemurro, Nicoletta Maratea, Colleen March, Jeff Murciniak, Jean Mariani, Brandi Marks, Lisa Maroccia, Renee Mastbaum, Brad Mayer, Brian McAlear, Claire McHugh, Katie McKenna, Carolyn Meehan, Denny Meelard, Johan Melendez, Alexis Mersel, James Michno, Danielle Mikol, Sheila Miller, Andrew Minder, Anna Miner, Kenia Montiho, Michael Morgan, Sarah Mott, Jeremy Munger, Grace Murphy, Anthony Nappi, Sharon Napurano, Adam Neri, Alice Ng, Fran Nicholas, Mary Beth Nigro, Jill Norton, Iyrenaah Novik, Kelly O'Connell, Megan O'Conner, Heather O'Kelly, James O'Leary, Laura Occhipinti, Chad Olszyk, Michael Panariello, Philip Rarisi, Jeff Park, Mehul Patel, Nittal Patel, Flank Patricia, Laurie Pedlar, Natalie Pereira, Maria Perez, Sherry Perez, Schubert Perotte, Oliver Peters, Michele Petrera, Craig Phares, Adam Phelps, Andrew Piccirillo, Elizabeth Piccoli, Brian Piekos, Veronique Pierre-Louis, Vickie Pistone, Lauren Porrovecchio, Axel Porter, Ashish Prasad, Susan Pries, Jill Prontnicki, Nicholas Puccio, Kelly Quigley, Neida Quinones, Robert Quinones, Alejandra Quintero, Rob Raike, Matt Rakowsky, Buddy Ramsey, John Reavey, Bobby Regan, Kerry Regan, Gautama Reid, Kevin Reid, Adam Reiffe, Cleauts Reynolds, Arno Rheinberger, Lam Rita, Mary Rivera, Therese Rizzo, Mario Roberti, Megan Robinson, Jessica Rosen, Jared Rosenbaum, Michele Rosenblum, Raquel Roxas, Shenise Rubi, Kira Rudnick, Richard Ruocco, Joao-Pierre Ruth, Janina Rzeszutek, Tarek Saleh, Vanessa Salomon, Heather Sams, Monica Santamaria, Richard Santos, Christine Savelli, John Scanlan, Laura Schaff, Smauel Schaffzin, Ruby Schein, Gemma Schettino, Julie Schick, Jaime Schiller, Alex Schmurdie, Robert Schroedley, Stuart Schultz, Melissa Schwartz, Erin Scott, Brad Screnci, Jeff Selinger, Jeff Seltzer, Pam Serman, Raquel Serouya, Joe Seybuck, Beth Shafer, Siddharth Shankar, Jessica Shannon, Renata Shaposhnikov, Swadesh Sharma, Melisa Sheffrin, Christine Sherwood, Jennifer Shilong, Jay Scultz, Alsion Shuman, Nabil Shurafa, Andrea Sibilia, Lori Silberman, Abigail Skillman, Nayan Sleth, Clint Smith, Colleen Smith, Muchelle Smith, Andrea Solecki, Kelly Sorce, Ligia Sorvillo, Margaret Stevens, Sheritte Stokes, Kathy Stott, Sarah Stuart, Christina Suzano, Jennifer Surich,, Rachel Swannell, Scott Sweet, Carol-Ann Szostak, Wendy Tait, Tom Tanis, David Tawil, Patty Teffennart, Wadeeah Terry, Andrea Tesch, John Thompson, Michael Tinello, Alfredo Torrado, Jeffrey Tyndall, Luisa Uribe, Regina Usrjat, Behrang Vali, Lilliana Vallejo, Timothy Vanvliet, Erika Vargas, Paula Vasquez, Mohnoush Vaziri, Max Veasy, Craig Verpeut, Mark Vinci, Lori Walbert, Amy Waldeyer, Brian Walsh, Ian Wasek, Stacey Weber, Kevin Weiner, Deborah Weintraub, Wendi Wesigarber, Marisa Weissman, Steven Widdowson, Caroline Willard, Elizabeth Williams, Billy Wingren, Aislyn Wist, Cahlin Wittreich, Heather Wolback, Tony Wong, Leah Workmen, Rich Wurst, Vivian Yee, Eric Yorker, David Zwillinger

Order Form

To order additional copies of *The Rutgers Students Unofficial Guide to College*, complete the following:

Name_____

Address_____

_____

City _____ State ____ Zip _____

Make checks payable to Arm in Arm Publishing for $9.95 per book plus $4.00 shipping and handling for the first book and $2.00 for each additional book.

Send payment and form (original or photocopy) to:

Arm in Arm Publishing, Inc
PO Box 996
East Brunswick, NJ 08816-9998

- -

We would be very happy to hear from you and welcome any additional comments, questions, or suggestions you might have. Send them to:

Arm in Arm Publishing
PO Box 996
East Brunswick, NJ 08816-9998